STEPS

GOSPEL-CENTERED RECOVERY

Mentor Guide

MATT CHANDLER
MICHAEL SNETZER

LifeWay Press®
Nashville, Tennessee

ISBN 978-1-4300-5343-9 • Item 005784029

Dewey decimal classification: 248.84 • Subject headings: DISCIPLESHIP / CHRISTIAN LIFE / SIN

Scripture quotations are taken from The Holy Bible, English Standard Version® (ESV®), copyright © 2001 by Crossway, a publishing ministry of Good News Publishers. Used by permission. All rights reserved. Scripture quotations marked NIV are taken from the Holy Bible, NEW INTERNATIONAL VERSION®. Copyright © 1973, 1978, 1984 by Biblica Inc. All rights reserved worldwide. Used by permission.

To order additional copies of this resource, write to LifeWay Resources Customer Service; One LifeWay Plaza; Nashville, TN 37234-0113; fax 615.251.5933; phone toll free 800.458.2772; order online at *www.lifeway.com;* email *orderentry@lifeway.com;* or visit the LifeWay Christian Store serving you.

Printed in the United States of America

Groups Ministry Publishing • LifeWay Resources • One LifeWay Plaza • Nashville, TN 37234-0152

Contents

Introduction to *Steps* Discipleship

Jesus came and said to them, "All authority in heaven and on earth
has been given to me. Go therefore and make disciples of all nations,
baptizing them in the name of the Father and of the Son and of the
Holy Spirit, teaching them to observe all that I have commanded you.
And behold, I am with you always, to the end of the age."
MATTHEW 28:18-20

The mission of *Steps* fits into the church's greater mission of bringing glory to God
by making disciples through gospel-centered worship, gospel-centered community,
gospel-centered service, and gospel-centered multiplication. *Steps* is an intensive
discipleship program that consists of daily Bible study and reflection, one-on-one
mentoring, sharing in small groups, and a large-group teaching time. We should not
view *Steps* as an attempt to climb a staircase to God through a religious system but
rather as steps of obedience in faithful response to what the gospel has already
accomplished and promised.

No one can lay a foundation other than that which is laid, which is
Jesus Christ. Now if anyone builds on the foundation with gold, silver,
precious stones, wood, hay, straw—each one's work will become
manifest, for the Day will disclose it, because it will be revealed by
fire, and the fire will test what sort of work each one has done.
1 CORINTHIANS 3:11-13

Steps begin by laying a foundation of all the gospel accomplishes for those who
believe (gospel truths) and then bid people to live out the call to follow Christ (gospel
pursuits). To clarify, we are not attempting to legitimize the 12 Steps as presented in
traditional, nongospel recovery contexts. However, we will examine and deconstruct
each step, claim whatever truth it may hold, reconstruct that truth within a biblical
framework, and apply it within a gospel context. To this end we have developed
Redeemed Truths.

This mentor guide is designed to help you proclaim the gospel to people who are
hurting and broken. The following pages will equip you to take a participant through
his or her assessment. It is recommended that you read the entire mentor guide all the
way through to familiarize yourself with the process and the materials. You can then
use it as a step-by-step guide while you listen to and process someone's assessment.

Truth and Pursuit

The message of the gospel is both comfort and call. It presents the comforting truth that in Christ we have been forgiven and made righteous. We are now sons and daughters of God and accepted into His kingdom for eternity, not because of any worth or work of our own but because of the loving choice of the Father and the sacrifice of the Son.

The gospel also offers us, as citizens of the kingdom, a call—a call to come and die, to forsake everything for the expansion of the kingdom of God, and to push back what is dark in the world. This call bids us to throw off the old self and clothe ourselves with the new self.

Gospel Truths
(Indicatives)

Gospel Pursuits
(Imperatives)

The structure of *Steps* addresses both the comfort and the call of the gospel message. Weeks 1–4 proclaim gospel truths (comfort), while weeks 5–12 begin to incorporate the importance of gospel pursuits (call).

WEEKS 1–4: GOSPEL TRUTHS

- The nature and character of God
- The fall
- Redemption
- Grace
- Faith and justification
- Adoption
- Sanctification
- Future glory

WEEKS 5–12: GOSPEL PURSUITS

- Holiness
- Reconciliation
- Spiritual disciplines
- Making disciples
- Gospel-centered worship
- Gospel-centered community
- Gospel-centered service
- Gospel-centered multiplication

The Assessment Process

The assessment process includes both the rooting out of sin and the replanting of biblical truth.

The goal in assessment is not for participants to identify every sin they have ever committed but to illuminate dysfunctional (sinful) patterns of relating to God and others. We want to be free of the things that rob our affections for Christ and hinder our ability to live for His kingdom purposes. Through this process we want to teach participants how to examine their hearts.

ASSESSMENT IS:
- Examining our hearts, guided by the Holy Spirit
- Being able to identify our sins and the sinful patterns behind them

ASSESSMENT IS NOT:
- An attempt to document every sin
- A one-time event

It is important to root ourselves in the gospel as we examine the darkness of our hearts. We begin by standing in the truths of the gospel—what Christ accomplished, what He is accomplishing, and what He promises to accomplish. We ask the Holy Spirit to reveal areas that hinder us from properly relating to God and others as ambassadors to a lost and dying world. We spend time writing what He reveals in our assessment. We must continually remember the gospel, believe the gospel, and stand in the gospel so that the Enemy does not cause us to stumble.

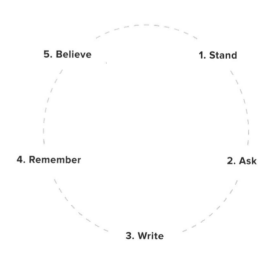

5. Believe

1. Stand

4. Remember

2. Ask

3. Write

An Overview of the Process

Examine Fruit	Confess and Pray	Expose Roots	Replant and Renounce	Encourage to Faithful Action

PHASE 1: EXAMINE FRUIT (WEEKS 5–7)

> When you were slaves of sin, you were free in regard to righteousness. But what fruit were you getting at that time from the things of which you are now ashamed? For the end of those things is death. But now that you have been set free from sin and have become slaves of God, the fruit you get leads to sanctification and its end, eternal life. For the wages of sin is death, but the free gift of God is eternal life in Christ Jesus our Lord.
>
> **ROMANS 6:20-23**

Traditional step 4: We made a searching and fearless moral assessment of ourselves.

Redeemed truth from step 4: As children of God armed with the Holy Spirit and standing firm in the gospel, we engage in the spiritual battle over the reign and rule of our hearts. God set us apart for holiness, and we look to put to death the areas of our lives that keep us from reflecting Jesus Christ to a dark and dying world. We first examine the fruit in our lives (or moral symptoms). As we move through the assessment process, we will uncover the roots of any ungodly fruit (pride and idolatry) that drive our ungodly thoughts, actions, and emotions.

In phase 1 participants should fill out the lighter shaded areas of the assessment forms. The forms illuminate the fruit of a person's thoughts, actions, and beliefs. There are six forms (two for each week during weeks 5–7): Abuse, Anger and Resentment, Guilt and Shame, Sexual Immorality, Fear, and Grief. Participants should complete and share these forms with their mentors (phase 2) during these weeks.

PLEASE NOTE: Mentors should check that all sections are complete, except those in dark blue, which they will complete with the participant.

PHASE 2: CONFESS AND PRAY (WEEKS 5–7)

If we say we have fellowship with him while we walk in darkness,
we lie and do not practice the truth. But if we walk in the light,
as he is in the light, we have fellowship with one another,
and the blood of Jesus his Son cleanses us from all sin.
1 JOHN 1:6-7

After you check for completeness, the participant should begin reading their assessment to you. As they read, allow this to be their time for simple confession—both to you and to God. During this phase you should refrain from pointing out their faults or from giving advice. It is a time to listen and pray. There is power in the simple act of bringing things out of the dark and into the light.

Traditional step 5: We admitted before God, ourselves, and another human being the exact nature of our wrongs.

Redeemed truth from step 5: Under the covering of God's grace, we step out in faith, leaving behind our old, self-protective ways of covering sin and hiding from God. We prayerfully come into the light, confessing our sins before God and to one another so that we may be healed.

As the participant confesses each item on the assessment, use the prayer prompts to help them pray about each issue or person. We have also provided two pages for taking notes. We recommend that you take notes to use during phases 3 and 4.

PHASE 3: EXPOSE ROOTS (WEEK 8)

No good tree bears bad fruit, nor again does a bad tree bear
good fruit, for each tree is known by its own fruit. For figs are not
gathered from thornbushes, nor are grapes picked from a bramble
bush. The good person out of the good treasure of his heart
produces good, and the evil person out of his evil treasure produces
evil, for out of the abundance of the heart his mouth speaks.
LUKE 6:43-45

By examining the various columns on each assessment form, you will help the participant uncover roots of pride, idolatry, and spiritual adultery that are causing the sinful fruit of their lives.

PHASE 4: REPLANT TRUTH AND RENOUNCE LIES (WEEK 8)

This phase of assessment deals with the spiritual dynamics behind the character defects, lies, and vows we consciously or unconsciously believed, pronounced, or entered. We come out of agreement with the Enemy and prayerfully set our intentions on reflecting Jesus to the world.

> ... assuming that you have heard about him and were taught in him, as the truth is in Jesus, to put off your old self, which belongs to your former manner of life and is corrupt through deceitful desires.
> **EPHESIANS 4:21-22**

Traditional step 6: We are entirely ready to have God remove all these defects of character.

Traditional step 7: We humbly asked Him to remove our shortcomings.

Redeemed truth from steps 6 & 7: In attempting to live independent of God, we have developed dysfunctional (sinful) patterns of coping. After careful examination we have begun to see the demonic roots of our slavery to these sinful patterns. We desire freedom. We renounce our former ways; offer ourselves to God; and, under the waterfall of His grace, ask Him to deliver and heal us by the authority of Christ and the power of the Holy Spirit. We also pray for blessing and the empowerment of the Holy Spirit to live life according to His kingdom purposes.

Using the sample guide provided, you will help the participant identify these lies, vows, and sinful patterns and then pray with them.

PHASE 5: ENCOURAGE TO FAITHFUL ACTION (WEEKS 9–12)

> Walk in a manner worthy of the Lord, fully pleasing to him, bearing fruit in every good work and increasing in the knowledge of God.
> **COLOSSIANS 1:10**

Through confession, prayer, counsel, and deliverance, the participant has worked to expel the sins, wounds, and oppressive powers that hinder their ability to "walk in a manner worthy of the Lord." It is now time to encourage the participant toward reconciliation, community, and obedience. You will help them create a list of persons with whom they need to reconcile.

Traditional step 8: We made a list of all persons we had harmed and became willing to make amends to them all.

Traditional step 9: We made direct amends to such people whenever possible, except when to do so would injure them or others.

Redeemed truth from steps 8 & 9: Relationships break down because of sin. If there were no sin in the world, relationships would work harmoniously, evidenced by love and unity. Division among God's people provides opportunities to identify sin and purify the body. The gospel of Jesus Christ brings about justice in a way that the law cannot by inwardly reconciling the very heart of injustice to God. As those forgiven by God, we can humbly approach those affected by our sin and make amends. This change of heart brings glory to God by demonstrating the power of the gospel and reflecting His heart in bringing justice through His reconciled people.

Additional redeemed truth from steps 8 & 9: As ambassadors of Christ, we are to be instruments of grace as we confront those who sin against us. We hand our offenses over to God and extend eager forgiveness to those who ask for it. And in this way, fellowship with God and among His people is preserved.

Traditional step 10: We continued to take personal inventory and, when we were wrong, promptly admitted it.

Traditional step 11: We sought through prayer and meditation to improve our conscious contact with God, praying only for the knowledge of His will and the power to carry that out.

Redeemed truth from steps 10 & 11: We continue in the fear of the Lord, putting to death those things that rob our affections for Christ while persevering in our loving and joyful obedience to Him. We return to the Lord quickly with an attitude of repentance, when out of step with the Spirit, as we're trained in godliness and grow spiritually. Since He is our ultimate treasure, we seek to know Him and fill ourselves with those things that stir our affections for Him. We practice spiritual disciplines so that our hearts, so prone to wander, might stay in rhythm with His.

Traditional step 12: Having had a spiritual experience as the result of these steps, we try to carry this message to others and to practice these principles in all our affairs.

Redeemed truth from step 12: Before the foundations of the earth, God chose us, the church, to live as messengers of reconciliation to a lost and dying world, bearing witness to His wisdom and power through the gospel of Jesus Christ. It is our joy-filled worship to make much of His name, empowered by the Holy Spirit in bringing a comprehensive gospel demonstrated by our deeds and proclaimed by our words, with the goal of making disciples for Jesus Christ. In this same way, we incarnate Christ, being His hands and feet on the earth.

TIME FRAME FOR COMPLETING ASSESSMENTS

The goal of this process is not to have an hour-long counseling session over each line of assessment. It should not take months to complete the process. The expectation is for mentors to meet weekly with their participants. We recommend one of the following options. (This time is in addition to the review of the Going Deeper questions in weeks 1–4 and 8–12.)

OPTION 1 (RECOMMENDED): Schedule three hours per week during weeks 5–7 (two assessments per week) to complete phase 2, then two hours in week 8 for phases 3–4, one hour to apply weeks 9–10, and one hour to develop an after-care plan for the participant.

OPTION 2: Schedule an entire day to work through phase 2 instead of three separate sessions during weeks 5–7, then two hours in week 8 for phases 3–4, one hour to apply weeks 9–10, and one hour to develop an after-care plan for the participant.

Choose the schedule that works best for you, the participant, and the ministry format. Each can be effective as long as you complete the entire process.

The Mentor Role, Expectations, and Accountability

Jesus came and said to them, "All authority in heaven and on earth has been given to me. Go therefore and make disciples of all nations, baptizing them in the name of the Father and of the Son and of the Holy Spirit, teaching them to observe all that I have commanded you. And behold, I am with you always, to the end of the age."
MATTHEW 28:18-20

Steps is a very structured process of discipleship and, due to its brevity, requires competence, character, consistency, and commitment.

CHARACTERISTICS

Qualified mentors should possess the following characteristics.

- *Competence.* They have completed *Steps* and have been recommended to be a mentor.
- *Character.* They love Jesus. They love, speak, and act toward others in a way that is consistent with His character. They operate under His authority.
- *Consistency.* They attend training to make sure all mentors follow a consistent process. Another aspect of consistency is meeting regularly with the mentee.
- *Commitment.* They are committed to finish the process even if it extends beyond the study and to disciple their mentee.

A person who has not yet completed *Steps* is not necessarily unqualified to be a mentor and may exhibit many characteristics of being a mentor. Enlisting a mentor who has not yet completed *Steps* is permitted but not ideal. This may be necessary, especially the first time your church offers *Steps*. After completing at least one round of *Steps*, experienced and inexperienced mentors can be paired during the *Steps* process to help a new mentor become more qualified.

EXPECTATIONS

We have the following expectations for mentors.

- Attend the first week of *Steps* with mentees, meet small-group leaders, and exchange information (if applicable).
- Meet weekly with their mentees.
- Attend training as needed and/or required.
- All mentors, regardless of their level of experience, are required to attend the first training, where they will receive their guides and any specific details for this semester.
- Follow the guide for reviewing the Going Deeper questions and completing the assessments.
- Be accountable to coaches and leaders for character and expectations.
- Help develop a next-steps or after-care plan that specifically presents the picture of a growing disciple by emphasizing gospel-centered worship, gospel-centered community, gospel-centered service, and gospel-centered multiplication.

An Overview of Biblical Counseling

The following overview seeks to differentiate biblical counseling from other forms of counsel that the world offers. Because we bear an influence on the lives that God has entrusted to us as shepherds, we must ensure that our counsel is biblical. Biblical counseling is distinct because it is rooted in the Scriptures, is aimed at the heart with the gospel of Jesus Christ, and exhorts Christ followers with the greatest command.

Rooted in the Scriptures

Where is the one who is wise? Where is the scribe? Where is the debater of this age? Has not God made foolish the wisdom of the world?

1 CORINTHIANS 1:20

The words of the wise are like goads, and like nails firmly fixed are the collected sayings; they are given by one Shepherd. My son, beware of anything beyond these.

ECCLESIASTES 12:11-12

THE WISDOM OF GOD VERSUS THE WISDOM OF THE WORLD

Rightly understood, all wisdom can be categorized in one of two ways. The Bible defines these sources of wisdom as the wisdom of God and the wisdom of the world (see 1 Cor 1:20-21). These two sources of wisdom are actually two different worldviews. One worldview exalts God and His glory as utmost; the other elevates man and his concerns. These two viewpoints regard the other as foolish and stand in opposition to each other. Even some Christians have tried to find a middle ground between these two worldviews. Biblical counseling begins from a perspective rooted in the wisdom of God and is oriented around His glory.

The wisdom of God is displayed most clearly in Jesus Christ. All creation exists to bring Him glory. The wisdom of the world reinterprets our experiences and desires in a way that leads us away from God as we orient our lives primarily around ourselves. The wisdom of the world is limited because it is based in speculation. The wisdom of God is based in revelation. As such, all counsel that mentors provide should be rooted in the wisdom God has revealed in His Word.

THE RELATIONSHIP BETWEEN ROOT AND FRUIT

> Thus says the LORD:
> "Cursed is the man who trusts in man
>   and makes flesh his strength,
>   whose heart turns away from the LORD.
> He is like a shrub in the desert,
>   and shall not see any good come.
> He shall dwell in the parched places of the wilderness,
>   in an uninhabited salt land.
> Blessed is the man who trusts in the LORD,
>   whose trust is the LORD.
> He is like a tree planted by water,
>   that sends out its roots by the stream,
> and does not fear when heat comes,
>   for its leaves remain green,
> and is not anxious in the year of drought,
>   for it does not cease to bear fruit."
>
> **JEREMIAH 17:5-8**

As can be seen in the previous passage, the two responses Jeremiah described lead to radically different lives. One is fruitful, and the other is fruitless. The fruit of a person's life will reveal their roots. Those who put their trust in God and His Word are nourished by the living waters of Jesus Christ. Their lives will be characterized by peace and good fruit amid difficult circumstances. Those who trust in man and the world will experience chaos and desolation. Those who seek to counsel biblically will encourage trust and faith in God with the understanding that faithful obedience to the Lord flows from a heart reconciled to Him by faith in Jesus.

AIMED AT THE HEART

> The heart is deceitful above all things
>   and desperately sick;
>   who can understand it?
>
> **JEREMIAH 17:9**

TARGETING SYMPTOMS OR ROOT CAUSES

The Bible describes the heart as the seat of a person, from which our emotions, thoughts, and behaviors originate (see Mark 7:21-22). The heart is the wellspring of our lives that drives our motivations and desires. Because of sin our hearts are corrupt. Outside the gospel we live with an incurable spiritual heart disease. By God's grace, faith in Jesus brings a new heart with new desires. However, sin and its effects remain, hindering our ability to see God, ourselves, and our lives rightly. Therefore, we need counsel that addresses the fundamental commitments in our lives with the hope of the gospel.

Secular approaches to counseling often treat only symptoms, focusing on behavior, thoughts, and emotions while failing to address the deeper issues of the heart. Treating symptoms has been described as giving aspirin to someon for a headache caused by a brain tumor. It may relieve the headache for a time, but it does nothing to fix the brain tumor.

Thankfully, we are not left without hope. God understands our hearts and has given us insights in His Word to explain the inner workings of man. God pursues the hearts of His people and will not rest until He wins them entirely. The biblical counsel that group leaders provide should address the root causes of our problems, not our symptoms alone.

THE GOSPEL OF JESUS CHRIST

> To those who are called, both Jews and Greeks,
> Christ [is] the power of God and the wisdom of God.
> **1 CORINTHIANS 1:24**

The gospel of Jesus Christ is the unfolding plan of God to redeem a people for His glory. God's Word reveals that the cause of all human suffering is sin. Therefore, the counsel that group leaders provide exalts the supremacy of the gospel of Jesus Christ as our ultimate hope amid our sin and suffering. To that end we seek to connect the truths of the gospel to our everyday struggles so that we can rejoice in the transformative grace of Jesus.

EXHORTING WITH THE GREATEST COMMAND

> "Hear, O Israel: The Lord our God, the Lord is one. And you shall love the
> Lord your God with all your heart and with all your soul and with all your
> mind and with all your strength." The second is this: "You shall love your
> neighbor as yourself." There is no commandment greater than these.
> **MARK 12:29-31**

God has hardwired us for worship. It is an expression of our humanness. We worship what is uppermost in our affections. The question is not whether we worship but what we worship.

All sin stems from disordered desires. These desires lead to idolatry—the worship of anything other than God. When we sin, we declare that in that moment we love something more than we love God. We give worship that is rightly due Him to another.

Through the gospel we are given new hearts with the reordering of His creative design and the reorientation of our hearts in worship to Him. Gospel-centered worship is a response to the reality that in Christ we have been given all things—the greatest of these being God Himself. Biblical counsel exhorts Christians to pursue rightly ordered worship that spills over into faithful action. We are to be "doers of the word, and not hearers only" (Jas. 1:22).

BIBLICAL COUNSELING EXAMPLE: DEPRESSION

How can these elements of biblical counseling be applied to serious problems like depression? To think biblically about depression, we must first begin by developing a biblical anthropology, or a scriptural understanding of people and what influences them. From this we will see that while it is possible to be spiritually oppressed, physically defective, and pressed by the circumstances around us, we can respond by the Holy Spirit with trust and faith in Christ under God's sovereign rule.

A Biblical Anthropology of the Active and the Passive Heart

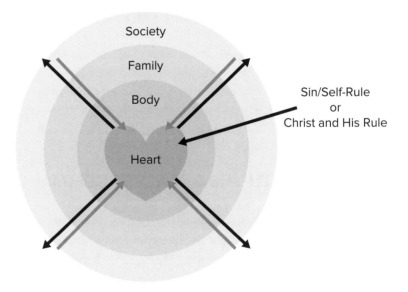

John Henderson, *Equipped to Counsel* (Bedford, TX: Association of Biblical Counselors, 2008).

From the diagram we see that there are physiological, social, and spiritual realities that can influence a person. Our physical bodies, the societies and cultures in which we live, and the unseen spiritual realm all influence our lives. Yet above it all God sits sovereignly enthroned, fully in control. He is sovereign over all things. Therefore, if we trust God in the midst of a chaotic situation, we will bear good fruit regardless of the source of the difficulty (see Jer. 17:7-8). If we place our trust elsewhere, we will be:

> like a shrub in the desert
> and shall not see any good come.
> **JEREMIAH 17:6**

This truth hints at the greater reality present as we counsel those who are struggling with depression. Despite the influences that surround us, the Bible focuses on the heart as the center of emotion, intellect, will, and desire. It is at the heart level that God ministers His grace to sufferers of depression.

One of the common features of depression is hopelessness. As you listen to others' stories of depression, you often hear evidence of misplaced hope. Many who struggle with depression say they have nothing left to live for. Their desires and dreams have gone unsatisfied. They feel lifeless, plunged into darkness. They have lost hope, motivation, and purpose. What a place for the gospel to enter!

In the greatest commandment Jesus exhorts us not to place our hope in lesser loves (see Mark 12:30). This is both for His glory and our good. In contrast to Jesus' words, depression often results from putting our hope in something other than God and His promise of redemption through the gospel of Jesus Christ. Because the world as we know it is passing away, finding our meaning in this world and the people of this world will leave us like Solomon, who, having it all, exclaimed, "Meaningless! Meaningless! ... Everything is meaningless! ... a chasing after the wind" (Eccl. 1:1-14, NIV).

We are told in Matthew 6:33:

> Seek first the kingdom of God and His righteousness,
> and all these things will be added to you.
> **MATTHEW 6:33**

In our natural, sinful state we seek the things we love—what we treasure. Jesus warns us that to treasure the things of the earth is to grasp for temporary, fleeting things that can never deliver on the security they promise. Instead, we are called to treasure and seek the eternal things of the kingdom of heaven.

We seek with our eyes, so if our eye is bad (when we seek temporary hopes and treasures), our whole body will be full of darkness. How great is that darkness outside the hope of the gospel! But if our eye is full of light, it brings light to the whole body. Through the gospel we have been given the eternal riches of the Kingdom. If someone is depressed, we want to invite that person to know the only One who brings light to the darkness, life from the dead, and order from chaos.

Even if there is a true chemical imbalance caused by a physical problem in our bodies or if there is spiritual oppression or social anxiety, our ministry to depressed people remains the same. We compassionately minister to the heart with the hope of the gospel of Jesus Christ amid all circumstances. There has never been a case of chemical imbalance (other than Jesus sweating blood in the garden of Gethsemane) that did not also expose heart issues that needed to be addressed.

This does not mean we discourage helpful symptomatic relief through medication or other means. It means we never want to lose sight that our real hope is not a chemical or a feeling. As Paul Tripp has said, "Hope is a person, and his name is Jesus Christ."[1] No matter how terrible a person feels, it is possible to look on our lives and situation with hope because of the light of the gospel of Jesus Christ.

These truths do not minimize or discount the very real and deep darkness of depression. God sees, and He cares. Because God is sovereign, He takes us into difficult seasons and uses them for good. There is a purpose for our suffering. Often the heart is exposed in seemingly never-ending forms of pride and idolatry, but through the gospel there is unending grace as God rescues us from the bondage of lesser hopes.

PLEASE NOTE: Additional Assessment Training can be downloaded from disc 1 of *Steps Bible Study Kit* or at *lifeway.com/steps.*

1. Paul Tripp, "Advent: The Promise" [online], 12 December 2012 [cited 2 October 2015]. Available from the Internet: *www.paultripp.com/wednesdays-word/posts/advent-the-promise.*

YOUR FIRST MEETING

Getting to Know Each Other

This meeting should take place before discussing week one of *Steps*.

▓ PRAY, LOVE, ASK, & LISTEN

Always open and close your time together in prayer. Be intentional about connecting organically with the person you are mentoring by asking about the week and showing genuine interest in the details of his or her life. Begin establishing a sense of trust by sharing about your own life. After this first meeting most of this time will be spent asking questions and listening. Always feel free take notes in the space provided.

Encourage discussion and ask questions to get to know each other. For example:

1. Share a little bit about yourselves (where you're from, personal interests, etc).
2. As a mentor, share your testimony and how God used *Steps* in your life.
3. Share with each other any positive or negative experiences in the past in regard to church or religion.
4. Empathize with hurts and emphasize your desire to help.
5. Share with each other what you hope to get from this one-on-one time and from *Steps* in general, including the group sessions, teaching, and personal study.

NOTES

_____

_____

_____

_____

_____

_____

_____

_____

_____

_____

■ SPEAK, LEAD, REMIND, & PRAY

It is important for those we disciple to see their problems biblically so that we can bring the hope of the gospel to their specific needs. You might feel tempted to think you must have answers to all their problems immediately. Keep your reflections for future sessions and for prayer. Introduce participants to Scriptures that speak to their circumstances. Remind them of their identity and of the promises and character of God.

Before concluding your meeting, be sure you both make note of the time and place you will meet next time.

As the participant is transparent and bares their soul, it is important that you cover them with the gospel in prayer as you conclude.

Schedule and Contact Information

PARTICIPANT'S NAME   CONTACT INFORMATION

DAY AND TIME OF MEETING   LOCATION

FREQUENCY OF MEETING (LIST DATES YOU WILL MEET)

LAYING A FOUNDATION

WEEK 1

Creation and Fall

◼ PRAY, LOVE, ASK, & LISTEN

Always open and close your time together in prayer. Be intentional about connecting organically with the person you are mentoring by asking about the week and showing genuine interest in the details of his or her life. Discuss the Going Deeper questions, taking notes as needed (this is a time to listen).

1. What do you think it means to fear the Lord?
2. Where does your heart go when you read the creation account?
3. Where does your heart go when you consider the suffering, pain, and hardship of our fallen world?
4. How does understanding God's pursuit and plan for redemption affect you?
5. According to the creation account, a functional human being is to live in a loving, dependent relationship with his Creator. In what areas of your life do you rely on creation rather than the Creator for direction, protection, provision, power, satisfaction, comfort, security, stability, hope, and happiness?
6. Describe your current suffering. What is the source?
7. God created us to be in loving relationships with Himself and others. Think about your close community and friends. Do you reach out to others when you need help? Why or why not? Where do they point you for hope?
8. In what ways do you disregard God's voice and follow another voice to pursue your own desires?
9. What do you do and where do you turn in your sin and suffering?
10. How do you attempt to remedy the problem? Or are you just defeated?

Review the redeemed truth for step 1 (see appendix A).

◼ SPEAK, LEAD, REMIND, & PRAY

It is important for those we disciple to see their problems biblically so that we can bring the hope of the gospel to their specific needs. You might feel tempted to think you have to have answers to all their problems immediately. Keep your reflections for future sessions and for prayer. Introduce participants to Scriptures that speak to their circumstances. Remind them of their identity and of the promises and character of God.

Before concluding your meeting, be sure you both make note of the next time and place you will meet next time.

As the participant is transparent and bares their soul, it is important that you cover them with the gospel in prayer as you conclude.

NOTES

The Remedy: The Gospel

■ PRAY, LOVE, ASK, & LISTEN

Ask whether the mentee has questions about the homework since the previous meeting.

Ask what the mentee learned about God and himself or herself this week.

Discuss the Going Deeper questions, taking notes as needed (this is a time to listen).

1. In what ways do you suppress the truth or live in denial (see Rom. 1:18)?
2. Do you find yourself acting like a rebellious lawbreaker or a self-righteous Pharisee? How does that tendency express itself in your life?
3. If the antidote to unrighteousness is not self-righteousness, what is it?
4. What about Christ and the gospel did you find beautiful this week?
5. To what or to whom did you look for hope and love in the past? In what or in whom did you place your trust?
6. How did Paul clarify what the Athenians worshiped as "the unknown god" (Acts 17:23)? What might be the dangers of a vague spirituality?
7. Scripture is clear: we must make a decision about our belief in Jesus. What hangs in the balance if we do nothing?
8. How have you responded to the invitation to trust in the Suffering Servant?
9. If you believe in Christ, describe how you came to believe.

Review the redeemed truth for step 2 (see appendix A).

■ SPEAK, LEAD, REMIND, & PRAY

NOTES

The Response: Repentance

▥ PRAY, LOVE, ASK, & LISTEN

Ask whether the mentee has questions about the homework since the previous meeting.

Ask what the mentee learned about God and himself or herself this week.

Discuss the Going Deeper questions, taking notes as needed (this is a time to listen).

1. If you have received the gift of faith, how has that led to a heartfelt desire to obey God?
2. Describe any experiences in which God's presence and power humbled you.
3. Describe ways the reality of God's love has affected your life.
4. Describe how you view God. What do you believe about His character, attributes, attitudes, and motivations?
5. What is your attitude toward God?
6. What is your view of humankind?
7. Define *repentance*. What has been your response to the call to repent? Why?
8. What evidence of spiritual rebirth do you see in your life?
9. Have you surrendered your life to Christ? If so, describe the process. If not, why?

Review the redeemed truth for step 3 (see appendix A).

▥ SPEAK, LEAD, REMIND, & PRAY

NOTES

WEEK 4

The Result: Justification, Adoption, and Sanctification

▓ PRAY, LOVE, ASK, & LISTEN

Ask whether the mentee has questions about the homework since the previous meeting.

Ask what the mentee learned about God and himself or herself this week.

Discuss the Going Deeper questions, taking notes as needed (this is a time to listen).

1. How do you tend to view suffering? How have the precious truths of Romans 8 shaped your views?
2. Paul rebuked the church in Galatia for trying to perfect themselves through human effort alone (works). How have you tried to overcome sin by trying harder instead of trusting the Holy Spirit's work in you (grace)? Explain the difference.
3. In what ways have you made excuses or placed blame for your ungodly thoughts, behaviors, and emotions (examples: family upbringing, suffering or loss, a medical or psychological diagnosis, "the Devil made me do it," blaming others)?
4. What grievous ways has God revealed to you?
5. Instead of presenting yourself for unrighteousness, how can you use the same effort, enthusiasm, and creativity to present yourself to God as an instrument of righteousness (see Rom. 6:13)?
6. What evidence of the Spirit of God do you see working in you?
7. What are your thoughts, concerns, and fears about completing your assessment?
8. What time will you set aside to complete your assessment? When will you meet with your mentor to share your assessment?
9. Why is it important to keep the gospel in full view as you dig into the dark places of your heart?

Review the redeemed truth for steps 4 and 5 (see appendix A).

▓ SPEAK, LEAD, REMIND, & PRAY

NOTES

ASSESSMENT

Before beginning the assessment process, reread the introduction
and overview on pages 6–11 in this mentor guide.

Additional Assessment Training can be downloaded from disc 1
of *Steps Bible Study Kit* or downloaded at *lifeway.com/steps*..

EXAMINE FRUIT

WEEKS 5–7

Phases 1 and 2 will be completed during weeks 5–7 according to the schedule below.

REMEMBER: Weeks 5–7 do not have Going Deeper discussion.

ASSESSMENT FORM DIRECTIONS AND DEFINITIONS

This section explains how the participant should fill out the assessment forms. It also defines the terms *abuse, resentment, guilt, shame, sexual immorality, fear,* and *grief* so that the participant and the mentor know what to include in each assessment.

ASSESSMENT FORMS

The participant will complete these forms:

> **WEEK 5: ABUSE**
> **ANGER AND RESENTMENT**
>
> **WEEK 6: SEXUAL IMMORALITY**
> **GUILT AND SHAME**
>
> **WEEK 7: FEAR**
> **GRIEF**

WHAT PART OF SELF WAS THREATENED?

This section explains the terms found in the assessment form so that the participant and the mentor know how to fill it out.

Assessment Form
Directions and Definitions

DIRECTIONS

1. Pray that the Holy Spirit reveals, leads, and comforts the participant as they fill out their assessment forms.
2. Instruct the participant to fill out the assessment forms vertically (column by column), not horizontally (row by row). It is easier to record everything when they fill them out this way. Staying in the same issue too long tends to become overwhelming.
3. Instruct the participant to fill out all light-blue spaces but to leave dark-blue spaces blank. They will complete the dark-blue spaces with you in phase 3 (during week 8).

REMEMBER: The participant will complete Phase 1 each week during weeks 5-7. You will be guiding the participant through Phase 2 in relation to the assessment forms filled out each week. Phase 2 will be a time for confession and prayer. Listening notes and prayer prompts related to each assessment are provided in Phase 2.

DEFINITIONS

ABUSE at its most basic level, is the misuse of anything. God created all things for His glory, and therefore, the misuse of His creation is abuse and ultimately sinful. All sin is abusive, and sin against others is undeserved. There are degrees of abuse that are horrific. For our purposes we want to limit our assessments to actions that are overtly abusive or have wounded us in a way that impairs the way we relate to God and others. Although abuse toward us undeserved, fruit such as fear, guilt, shame, and resentment often comes out of these tragedies.

RESENTMENT is a root of bitterness that takes hold in our hearts when we fail to entrust offenses to the Lord. Resentments can be both active (aggression) and passive (withdrawal) in nature. We often replay in our minds the situations involving people, principles, roles, and institutions.

SEXUAL IMMORALITY is any sexual act that occurs outside God's intended design for sex between one man and one woman within the marriage covenant. Beyond sexual acts, God looks deeper to the desires and motivations of the heart.

GUILT can be both a state and a feeling that occurs when we have violated a law or a moral standard. We can feel guilty and not be guilty (false guilt), or we can be guilty but not feel guilty. justice.

SHAME is the intense feeling of being unclean, defiled, and dirty. Closely related to guilt, shame may result from the exposure of a person's own sin and depravity or from sin committed against a person's dignity. Shame is deeply rooted in identity ("I am worthless; I am dirty").

FEAR is an emotional response to a perceived threat or danger. Healthy fear prompts a person to act in the face of imminent danger. We experience unhealthy fear when there is no imminent danger.

GRIEF is deep sorrow over the loss of someone or something we love. This includes people, relationships, safety, security, identity, possessions, affections, and desires.

ASSESSMENT FORMS

The assessment forms are modified and expanded from forms in *Joe and Charlie Big Book Study,* then viewed through a redemptive lens.

ABUSE ASSESSMENT FORM

Rejoice not over me, O my enemy; when I fall, I shall rise; when
I sit in darkness, the Lord will be a light to me. **MICAH 7:8**

Source	Cause	Type of Abuse					
		Sexual	Emotional	Power/authority	Ritualistic	Verbal	Physical

						My Response						
If any of these are currently present in my life regarding this situation, add to other assessments.							**Exact nature of my wrongs, faults, and mistakes (to complete with mentor)**					
Shame	Resentment	Fear/anxiety	Grief/loss	Guilt	Regarding guilt: renounce the lie that I am responsible for the abuse.		Self-centered	Self-seeking	Frightened	Dishonest	Inconsiderate	Other

ANGER AND RESENTMENT ASSESSMENT FORM

See to it that no one fails to obtain the grace of God; that no "root of bitterness" springs up and causes trouble, and by it many become defiled. **HEBREWS 12:15**

Source	Cause	Effect

What part of self was hurt or threatened?						Exact nature of my wrongs, faults, and mistakes (to complete with mentor)					
Social		Security									
Self-esteem	Personal relationships	Material	Emotional	Sexual	Ambitions	Self-centered	Self-seeking	Frightened	Dishonest	Inconsiderate	Other

NOTES

SEXUAL-IMMORALITY ASSESSMENT FORM

Flee from sexual immorality. ... Your body is a temple of the Holy Spirit. ... You are not your own,
for you were bought with a price. So glorify God in your body. **1 CORINTHIANS 6:18-20**

Who/What	Cause	Effect

What part of self was threatened or seeking satisfaction?						Exact nature of my wrongs, faults, and mistakes (to complete with mentor)					
Social		Security									
Self-esteem	Personal relationships	Material	Emotional	Sexual	Ambitions	Self-centered	Self-seeking	Frightened	Dishonest	Inconsiderate	Other

NOTES

_____

_____

_____

_____

_____

_____

_____

_____

_____

_____

_____

_____

_____

_____

_____

_____

_____

_____

_____

_____

_____

_____

_____

_____

_____

GUILT AND SHAME ASSESSMENT FORM

I do not nullify the grace of God, for if righteousness were through the law, then Christ died for no purpose. **GALATIANS 2:21**

Cause	Who Was Hurt?	Effect

What part of self was threatened or seeking satisfaction?						Exact nature of my wrongs, faults, and mistakes (to complete with mentor)					
Social		Security									
Self-esteem	Personal relationships	Material	Emotional	Sexual	Ambitions	Self-centered	Self-seeking	Frightened	Dishonest	Inconsiderate	Other

FEAR ASSESSMENT FORM

I, the LORD your God, hold your right hand; it is I who say to you, "Fear not, I am the one who helps you." **ISAIAH 41:13**

Fear	Effect

Circumstance

What influences or circumstances
contributed to this fear?

Where is my treasure?

(Complete with mentor.)

Review Matthew 6:19-34.

GRIEF ASSESSMENT FORM

"I have said these things to you, that in me you may have peace. In the world you will have tribulation. But take heart; I have overcome the world." **JOHN 16:33**

Who/What	Remember	Effect

What temptations have come from my suffering?									Exact nature of my wrongs, faults, and mistakes (to complete with mentor)					
Toward God		Toward Others		Toward Myself										
Doubt	Anger	Envy	Anger	Self-pity	Isolation	Guilt	Fear/anxiety	Denial	Self-centered	Self-seeking	Frightened	Dishonest	Inconsiderate	Other

What Part of Self Was Threatened?

These definitions will be useful to you and the participant in determining which part of self was hurt or threatened or was seeking satisfaction in the Resentment, Guilt & Shame, and Sexual Immorality assessments. Your participant should place a check mark in any boxes that apply.

DEFINITIONS

Did the following things threaten your desires, or did the desire for these things motivate your response?

SELF-ESTEEM: The desire for love, worth, and value

PERSONAL RELATIONSHIPS: The desire to belong and have meaningful relationships

MATERIAL SECURITY: The desire to feel materially secure or gain material wealth

EMOTIONAL SECURITY: The desire or drive for peace of mind and emotional security

SEXUAL RELATIONS/SEXUALITY: Sexual desires

AMBITIONS: Future plans and hopes in any of the previous areas

EXAMPLES

The following examples illustrate how to identify which part of self is being hurt or threatened.

RESENTMENT: "I am angry at my mother for taking me out of her will. I feel that she doesn't care about me [self-esteem] at all, and I was counting on that money to pay my debt [material security]. I am convinced that she loves my sister more than me [emotional security], and her favoritism has always caused my sister and me to be estranged [personal relationships]."

SEXUAL IMMORALITY: "When I watched pornography, it made me feel powerful [self-esteem] and met my sexual needs [sexual relations/sexuality]. It also allowed me intimacy without having to be vulnerable [emotional security]."

GUILT AND SHAME: "I feel shame over being raped. I feel worthless now, as if no one will ever love me [self-esteem]. Being raped has made it difficult to date [sexual relations/sexuality] because all I think about is how dirty I feel. I fear that I will never be able to have sex [sexual ambitions] in a healthy way."

CONFESS AND PRAY

WEEKS 5–7

Phase 2 is completed during weeks 5–7 and does not have Going Deeper discussion.

Use the following prayer prompts with the participant as you review the items on their assessments. A sample prayer is suggested that highlights theological truths about each issue. The participant can use the prayer or can say their own. If the participant uses their own words, it is important that they express the same truths. Accordingly, each sample prayer includes a list of the elements of that prayer to guide the participant.

REMEMBER: Phase 2 is a time for confession and prayer—for bringing things out of the darkness and into the light. You should take listening notes, but resist the temptation to immediately point out faults or give advice.

SUGGESTIONS FOR CONFESSION AND PRAYER

1. Begin with prayer.
    a. Invite Jesus into this intimate gathering. He is the only One who has the power to heal.
    b. Ask that you will encounter truth and that the Holy Spirit will bring healing and freedom.
    c. Ask for wisdom and protection.
    d. Ask God to silence the voice of the Enemy.

2. Ask the participant if they purposefully left anything off their assessment. If so, give them an opportunity to bring that item into the light.

3. Listen to the participant as they confess the items on their assessment, using the space provided on the following pages to make notes as needed.

4. Lead the participant in prayer.

Abuse

LISTEN FOR AND MAKE NOTE OF:

1. *Lies the participant seems to believe.* Some examples may include: "If they had not done this, I would be OK." "The abuse was my fault." "The abuse was God's fault." "I deserved it." "I am dirty." Other lies might be that God had forsaken them during the abuse, not realizing that God intervened by sending His Son. Also listen for the lies within Satan's seduction (see Gen. 3:1-6), like "I can't trust God." "I am the only one who can be trusted." "I can be my own God." "It is no big deal."

2. *Sinful patterns in response to abuse.* For example, a child has no role in the abuse they suffered. They did not cause it, and they did not deserve it. In many cases there was nothing the child could have done to prevent it. However, when that same child grows up and uses that abuse to justify sin, rebellion, and distrust of the Lord, they are responding sinfully. Examples of sinful responses to note:

   - Taking responsibility for what is not theirs and not taking responsibility for what is theirs
   - Refusing to trust God or others
   - Using sex to control—sex as a weapon instead of a weakness
   - A fear or hatred of sexuality, which is a good gift from God
   - Taking revenge or fantasizing about it
   - Constantly living in a victim mentality
   - Various forms of self-protection, including isolation, idolizing safety, hypervigilance to potential harm, disassociation
   - Killing good, God-given desires and thinking, *If I did not desire these things, then I would not be hurt.*
   - Manipulating others for their affection from a fear they will leave
   - Being resistant to heal so as not to lose the justification to sin
   - Other character defects (see appendix E)

3. *Areas that need healing.*

4. *Areas in which the participant needs to take faithful action.* These may include confession, amends, or biblical confrontation.

Lies/vows

....
....
....
....
....
....
....
....
....
....
....
....
....
....

Areas that need healing

....
....
....
....
....
....
....
....
....
....
....
....
....
....

Sinful patterns/character defects

....
....
....
....
....
....
....
....
....
....
....
....
....
....

Faithful action needed

....
....
....
....
....
....
....
....
....
....
....
....
....
....

PRAYER PROMPTS

Abuse

After the participant completes their assessment, confessing to God and to you, pray over them. Prior to having the participant pray, walk them through the prayer below. They may pray the prayer as written or use the elements of the prayer in their own words.

PLEASE NOTE: Pray through each item, person, or circumstance in the assessment.

PRAYER FOR ABUSE

Heavenly Father, I thank You that You are the God who sees. I thank You that when _____ [name abuser] _____ [name abuse], You were there. I thank You that when no one else heard my cries, You did. You sent Your Son to this world to rescue me and give me life. Jesus, You know well my pain, because You Yourself suffered much at the hands of sinners. I pray that You will teach me through your Spirit to love as You love. Thank You for rescuing me from the dominion of darkness and bringing me with You into eternity. I thank You that I am no longer a victim but more than a conqueror through the cross. In Christ I am cleansed. I pray, in the name of Jesus Christ, that You will heal any emotional, spiritual, mental, relational, or physical damage done as a result of this abuse in my life, as well as any other people affected, for Your glory and Your namesake. Help me not to focus on the way people have treated me but instead on what You have given me. Show me how to be an instrument of Your redeeming love in this situation. [Take a moment to pray for the abuser.] In Jesus' name, amen.

ELEMENTS OF THIS PRAYER

- Acknowledge that God sees, knows, and cares about our darkest moments.
- Thank Him that He sent Christ to rescue us.
- Acknowledge that Christ understands, because He Himself suffered, and that the Holy Spirit will teach you to love as He loves.
- Thank God that we are no longer enslaved to darkness and that we will spend eternity with Him.
- Acknowledge that we are more than conquerors in Christ (see Rom. 8:37) and are no longer victims.
- Pray for healing.
- Ask God to help you focus on what you have been given eternally rather than on what has been taken from you in this life.
- Pray for wisdom in being an instrument of His redeeming love in this situation.
- Pray for the abuser.

LISTENING NOTES

Resentment

LISTEN FOR AND MAKE NOTE OF:

1. *Lies the participant seems to believe.* Example: "If I forgive them, they will get away with this."

2. *Patterns of sin and sinful responses.* Examples include:

   - Putting unrealistic expectations on a person and becoming resentful when they fail you
   - Judging or being angry over things that you yourself do
   - Using judgment as a means of elevating yourself or making yourself feel better about your sins
   - Being passive-aggressive. Many people feel resentment, but in their pride they refuse to acknowledge their anger in order to save face.
   - Other character defects (see appendix E)

3. *Areas that need healing.*

4. *Areas in which the participant needs to take faithful action.* These may include confession, amends, or biblical confrontation.

Lies/vows

....
....
....
....
....
....
....
....
....
....
....
....
....
....

Areas that need healing

....
....
....
....
....
....
....
....
....
....
....
....
....
....

Sinful patterns/character defects

....
....
....
....
....
....
....
....
....
....
....
....
....

Faithful action needed

....
....
....
....
....
....
....
....
....
....
....
....
....

PRAYER PROMPTS

Resentment

After the participant confesses their assessment, pray over them. Prior to having the participant pray, walk them through the prayer below. They may pray the prayer as written or use the elements of the prayer in their own words.

PLEASE NOTE: Pray through each item, person, or circumstance in the assessment.

PRAYER FOR RESENTMENT TOWARD OTHERS

Heavenly Father, I acknowledge that [person's name] is not exempt from the fall and the effects of sin. Though I do not like the symptoms of this spiritual disease or the ways it has affected me, he [or she], like me, is a sinner. I confess that I have stood in judgment of _____ for _____. Forgive me, Father, for allowing bitterness and resentment to reside in my heart, preventing my ability to be an instrument of Your redeeming love. As You, Father, have extended your grace to me through Jesus Christ, I ask the Holy Spirit to enable me to reflect Christ in this situation. Today I, as an unrighteous judge, turn this offense over to you, my righteous Judge and King. I trust in Your will and Your plan and choose to live in the freedom You have promised. How may I be an ambassador of your love, peace, and truth in this situation? I pray in the name of Jesus Christ that You will, for Your namesake and glory, heal any damage done as a result of this offense in my life, as well as any others who may have been affected. [Finish your prayer by praying for this person according to his or her needs.] In Jesus' name, amen.

ELEMENTS OF THIS PRAYER

- Humble yourself as a fellow sinner.
- Confess specific resentment.
- Ask for forgiveness for harboring bitterness .
- Ask for the Holy Spirit's help in being Christlike.
- Turn the offense over to God.
- Ask for wisdom on how to best steward this relationship for God's kingdom purposes.
- Pray for healing.
- Pray for the person.

PRAYER FOR RESENTMENT TOWARD SELF

Heavenly Father, forgive me for the ways I have attempted to find righteousness apart from the work of Your Son. By standing outside myself, elevating myself and judging myself for my actions, emotions, and behavior and therefore hating myself, I have attempted to deal with my shortcomings according to the law rather than Your grace. I tend to punish myself when I break my standards, seeking some sense of justification. In doing so, I try to deal with my sin independent of You and remain in self-imposed bondage. I have placed myself above You as judge. Today I come humbly before You so that I can come under the waterfall of Your grace. Thank You for Your Son, Jesus, and the freedom that grace brings. In Jesus' name, amen.

ELEMENTS OF THIS PRAYER
- Ask for forgiveness for attempting to find righteousness apart from Christ.
- Confess attempts to deal with shortcomings according to the law rather than grace.
- Repent of punishment and judgment of yourself in an attempt to seek justification.
- Acknowledge the self-imposed bondage you have created in attempting to deal with your sin apart from Christ.
- Ask to stand under His grace and the freedom He brings.
- Give thanksgiving for Jesus.

PRAYER FOR RESENTMENTS TOWARD GOD

Heavenly Father, I confess my resentment toward You for _____. I ask Your forgiveness for my pride, standing in judgment of a good, perfect, just, and holy God who can see the eternal perspective, while I can see only what is right before me. Help me, by the power of Your Holy Spirit, to trust You and remember that Your plans are to bless me and not to harm me, to give me hope and a future. In Jesus' name, amen.

ELEMENTS OF THIS PRAYER
- Confess specific resentment.
- Ask for forgiveness for standing in judgment.
- Humbly acknowledge that you do not knows what God knows.
- Repent of not trusting God and His eternal perspective.
- Give thanksgiving for the assurance God provides His children.

LISTENING NOTES

Sexual Immorality

LISTEN FOR AND MAKE NOTE OF:

1. *Lies the participant seems to believe.* Examples:

   - Believing that sex is bad or dirty
   - Believing that sex is a purely physical act with no spiritual or emotional consequences
   - Believing that one's worth is defined by their ability to give sexual pleasure

2. *Sinful patterns in dealing with sex.* Examples:

   - Taking on an oversexualized personality
   - Attempting to gain power and control that were lost: "If I give it away, then it can never be taken from me" or "Sex will be my weapon instead of my weakness."
   - Using sex as a form of emotional or physical domination—a way to exercise power over another person
   - Placing blame on another person for sexual sin. For example: "I was seduced." "He lied to me." Although those statements may be true, two people who had consensual sex with each other have sinned.
   - A failure to recognize sex as an act of worship, often desiring self-exaltation to such a degree that you are willing to defile another person to get it
   - A failure to recognize that seducing someone with your body to get affection is a form of prostitution—using your body to get something you desire
   - A failure to recognize that participation in prostitution, escorts, or strip clubs is a degrading and dignity-robbing practice that reduces a human being, who is made in the image of God, to a base object for sexual pleasure
   - Other character defects (see appendix E)

3. *Areas that need healing.*

4. *Areas in which the participant needs to take faithful action.* These may include confession, amends, or biblical confrontation.

Lies/vows

....
....
....
....
....
....
....
....
....
....
....
....
....
....

Areas that need healing

....
....
....
....
....
....
....
....
....
....
....
....
....
....

Sinful patterns/character defects

....
....
....
....
....
....
....
....
....
....
....
....
....
....

Faithful action needed

....
....
....
....
....
....
....
....
....
....
....
....
....
....

Sexual Immorality

After the participant confesses their assessment, pray over them. Prior to having the participant pray, walk them through the prayer below. They may pray the prayer as written or use the elements of the prayer in their own words.

PLEASE NOTE: Pray through each item, person, or circumstance in the assessment.

PRAYER FOR SEXUAL IMMORALITY

Heavenly Father, I realize that sex is sacred. It is a beautiful picture of oneness reserved exclusively for one man and one woman within the context of the marriage covenant. Sex is a gift from You that is intended to glorify You. It is the mingling of souls. Lord, I confess today that I have sinned and operated outside Your intended design for this holy endeavor by _____. Father, forgive me. I have given intimate parts of myself to another. Lord, I long to glorify You. I ask that You will restore to me a right view of sex. I pray, in the name of Jesus Christ, that for Your namesake and by Your power, You will heal the damage done as a result of this situation in my life, as well as any damage in other lives that have been affected. I pray You will sever any soul ties related to this sin. I trust in the redemptive work of Christ and His covering for my shame. I pray that You will remove or help me take captive the images and emotions tied to these events and prevent me from fantasizing or taking pride in things that grieve Your heart. Through the cross of Christ I am made clean. In Jesus name', amen.

ELEMENTS OF THIS PRAYER

- Acknowledge the sacred beauty and gift that sex is within its intended design.
- Acknowledge the spiritual reality that takes place when two people join together.
- Confess sin specifically.
- Ask for forgiveness.
- Express your desire to bring glory to God.
- Pray for a restored view of sex.
- Pray for healing.
- Pray for the breaking of soul ties.
- Express trust in God's work in you.
- Ask for help in taking your thoughts captive, making them obedient to the will of Christ, and ask for the removal of images and emotions related to the event.
- Acknowledge having been cleansed through the blood of Jesus.

LISTENING NOTES

Guilt and Shame

LISTEN FOR AND MAKE NOTE OF:

1. *Lies the participant seems to believe.* Example: "I can never be forgiven for this" or "I am dirty."

2. *Sinful patterns of dealing with guilt and shame.* Examples:

   - Attempts to redeem self apart from Christ through works
   - Being a perfectionist
   - Self-sabotage—stop trying in order to avoid failing
   - Deflection—avoiding the issue
   - Self-condemnation—an attempt to justify themselves
   - Condemnation of others—judging others in an attempt to remedy their own shame
   - Unwillingness to walk in transparency or to trust others
   - Telling others inappropriate, intimate information in an attempt to test them to see if they will leave
   - Other character defects (see appendix E)

3. *Areas that need healing.*

4. *Areas in which the participant needs to take faithful action.* These may include confession, amends, or biblical confrontation.

Lies/vows

....
....
....
....
....
....
....
....
....
....
....
....
....
....

Areas that need healing

....
....
....
....
....
....
....
....
....
....
....
....
....
....

Sinful patterns/character defects

....
....
....
....
....
....
....
....
....
....
....
....
....
....

Faithful action needed

....
....
....
....
....
....
....
....
....
....
....
....
....
....

Guilt and Shame

After the participant confesses their assessment, pray over them. Prior to having the participant pray, walk them through the prayer below. They may pray the prayer as written or use the elements of the prayer in their own words.

PLEASE NOTE: Pray through each item, person, or circumstance in the assessment.

PRAYER FOR GUILT AND SHAME (AS A RESULT OF OUR SIN)

Heavenly Father, today I confess that my attempts to deal with my guilt and shame by covering them with the works of my hands and hiding in darkness have failed. I come before Your throne and ask for Your forgiveness for [name the sin]. I thank You that when I come before You, hiding nothing, and trust solely in the sufficiency of Christ, I receive the covering of Your grace. I pray in the name of Jesus Christ that, by Your power, You will heal the damage done in my life as a result of this situation, as well as any damage in other lives that have been affected, and lead me to faithful reconciliation in this situation. In Jesus' name, amen.

ELEMENTS OF THIS PRAYER
- Confess the attempt to deal with guilt and shame apart from the cross of Christ.
- Confess sin and ask for forgiveness.
- Acknowledge receiving God's grace and express gratitude for the sufficiency of Christ's payment.
- Pray for the healing and restoration of the other people affected.
- Ask what needs to be done to rectify the situation.

When you receive God's forgiveness but fail to forgive yourself, you kick God off the throne and set yourself up as the higher authority. In essence you count the cross of Jesus as nothing. Repent and accept Christ's forgiveness. Walk in the freedom of knowing that Jesus' blood is sufficient. Thank Him.

PRAYER FOR SHAME (AS A RESULT OF ANOTHER'S SIN)

Heavenly Father, today I confess that my attempts to deal with my shame by covering it with the works of my hands and hiding in darkness have failed. Because I now trust in the cleansing work of the cross of our Lord Jesus Christ, I now step out of the darkness and into the light. Though _____ may have _____, there is nothing that the resurrecting power of Jesus cannot overcome. Through the cross of Christ I am made clean. I pray in the name of Jesus Christ that, by Your power, You will heal the damage done in my life as a result of this situation, as well as any damage in other lives that have been affected. In Jesus' name, amen.

ELEMENTS OF THIS PRAYER

- Acknowledge insufficiency in attempting to deal with shame apart from the cross of Christ.
- Bring to light the specific sin by naming the person and what he or she did.
- Acknowledge that there is no sin that the resurrection power of Christ cannot overcome.
- Acknowledge having been made clean through the cross of Christ.
- Pray for the healing of those affected.

Fear

LISTEN FOR AND MAKE NOTE OF:

1. *Lies the participant seems to believe that are motivating fear.*

2. *Evidence of idolatry, distrust, lust, and old wounds that may motivate their fears.*
   - Fear occurs when in our pride, we think we know what is best for us, and something begins to threaten that belief.
   - Fears reveal old wounds we have not allowed the Lord to heal.
     Example: "I am afraid of getting hurt again."
   - Fears reveal what we are trying to protect.
   - Fears reveal much about where we get our value and identity.
   - Fears can reveal our idols—what we are afraid to lose. We tend to fear losing the things we lust for.
   - Whatever you fear more than God will control and dominate you.
   - Other character defects (see appendix E)

3. *Areas that need healing.*

4. *Areas in which the participant needs to take faithful action.* These may include confession, amends, or biblical confrontation.

Lies/vows

....
....
....
....
....
....
....
....
....
....
....
....
....
....

Areas that need healing

....
....
....
....
....
....
....
....
....
....
....
....
....
....

Sinful patterns/character defects

....
....
....
....
....
....
....
....
....
....
....
....
....
....

Faithful action needed

....
....
....
....
....
....
....
....
....
....
....
....
....
....

PRAYER PROMPT

Fear

After the participant confesses their assessment, pray over them. Prior to having the participant pray, walk them through the prayer below. They may pray the prayer as written or use the elements of the prayer in their own words.

PLEASE NOTE: Pray through each item, person, or circumstance in the assessment.

PRAYER FOR FEAR

Heavenly Father, forgive me for walking in the fear of _____. I pray that You will help me trust You more. I acknowledge that when I fear, I cannot walk in love. I realize that self-preservation is at the root of my fears. In my pride I attempt to control my world and fail to trust in Your ability to preserve my life. I forget that You are a good God and are fully in control. Therefore, today I turn these fears over to You. I trust that You will meet all my needs as You promise, not always the way I want. I trust that the ups and downs of life have purpose and that through it all, You, Lord, never change. Thank You that You are always with me. In areas of my life where I have lived under the curse of fear, I pray that You will allow me the blessing of faith that comes through grace. In Jesus' name, amen.

ELEMENTS OF THIS PRAYER

- Ask for forgiveness.
- Confess fear.
- Ask for help in trusting God.
- Acknowledge your inability to walk in love when you fear.
- Acknowledge the roots of fears.
- Turn fears over to God.
- Place your trust in God and His goodness.
- Thank God for always being with you.
- Pray for blessings of faith in areas of your life where you have walked under the curse of fear.

LISTENING NOTES

Grief

LISTEN FOR AND MAKE NOTE OF:

1. *Lies the participant seems to believe.*

2. *Ways the participant may have responded sinfully in their attempts to handle their grief and loss apart from the Lord.* Sinful patterns of handling loss may include:
   - Repression of God-given desires in order to protect oneself from being hurt again
   - Bitterness toward God or others
   - Inability or unwillingness to enter the suffering—self-protection
   - Coveting what you lost in that person or thing, rooted in idolatry
   - Transfer to another object, leading to fear and control
   - Other character defects (see appendix E)

3. *Areas that need healing.*

4. *Areas in which the participant needs to take faithful action.* These may include confession, amends, or biblical confrontation.

Lies/vows

....
....
....
....
....
....
....
....
....
....
....
....
....
....

Areas that need healing

....
....
....
....
....
....
....
....
....
....
....
....
....
....

Sinful patterns/character defects

....
....
....
....
....
....
....
....
....
....
....
....
....
....

Faithful action needed

....
....
....
....
....
....
....
....
....
....
....
....
....
....

Grief

After the participant confesses their assessment, pray over them. Prior to having the participant pray, walk them through the prayer below. They may pray the prayer as written or use the elements of the prayer in their own words.

PLEASE NOTE: Pray through each item/person/circumstance in the assessment.

PRAYER FOR GRIEF

Father, I thank You that You are a God who hears my cries and wipes away my tears. My heart is weary and often wants to give in to despair. Give me strength and grace to believe the truth of Your character and Your Word. Increase my faith to believe that Your glory is worth this momentary affliction. Forgive me for times when I want my pain to disappear more than I want to draw near to You, even when I know You are the only One who can comfort me. I know You are the only One who can heal my broken heart and bind my wounds. Jesus, I trust You with my heart and my life because I believe in Your great love for me. Will You meet me here and walk me through this process of healing as I begin to let _____ go? Help me keep my eyes on You and Your eternal promises. [Pray and lament as you need to.] In Jesus' name, amen.

ELEMENTS OF THIS PRAYER

- Admit sorrow, hurt, grief, and pain.
- Thank God for His presence.
- Confess your tendency to seek comfort from the world rather than God.
- Acknowledge the Holy Spirit's ability to bring comfort.
- Trust God with your broken heart.
- Ask for healing.
- Ask for help.

EXPOSE ROOTS

WEEK 8

This week you will walk the mentee through phases 3 and 4 of the assessment and the Going Deeper questions found on page 87. Once complete, assessments can reveal areas of spiritual adultery, idolatry, and pride that are causing sinful fruit in their lives.

Who/What, Sources and Causes (Spiritual Adultery)	What Part of Self Was Threatened? (Idolatry)	Exact Nature of My Wrongs, Faults, and Mistakes (Pride/Flesh)

SPIRITUAL ADULTERY: Going to the world or to people for what only God can provide
How, where, and whom has this person been worshiping?

IDOLATRY: Elevating even good, God-given desires to ultimate importance
What has this person been demanding through spiritual adultery?

PRIDE: Attempting to live independent of God in gratifying fleshly desires
Is this person living in submission to God according to the Spirit?
Or are they living independent of God, seeking to gratify their flesh?

In the previous phase you prayed with the participant as he or she confessed the events, causes, and effects on their assessments. The final columns clarify responsibility and help the participant to view his or her assessments with spiritual eyes. The following pages will guide you through the darker columns of the assessment forms: The Exact Nature of My Wrongs, Faults, and Mistakes and What Part of Self Was Threatened?

Getting to the Roots of Ungodly Fruit and Character Defects

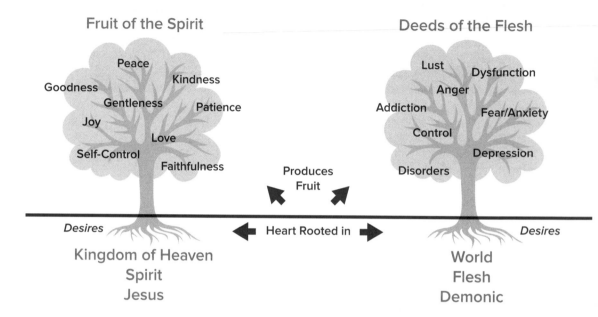

The Exact Nature of My Wrongs, Faults, and Mistakes

In order to see the roots beneath the surface of the ungodly fruit in a person's life, we will look to the way God's Word speaks to ungodly anger and fighting (see Jas. 4:1-10). This insight should help to see the roots of all ungodly fruit and character defects being unearthed through the assessment.

Ideally, weeks have been spent listening to the pain and heartache of a person's life as they have been brought before the Lord in prayer. Now it is time to approach the assessment from a different perspective by clarifying responsibilities. In part, that means renouncing the lie that sinful actions committed against the participant are their fault. Additionally, it means the participant must take responsibility for what is coming from their heart. Though an action toward them was not their fault, they are responsible for their response. Compare their response to Jesus' response. When we pursue even a godly desire in a sinful way, the result is selfish, dishonest, and fearful behavior.

Begin by leading the participant to fill out the "Exact nature of my wrongs, faults, and mistakes" section of their assessments.

SELFISH/SELF-CENTERED

Does my response stem from how something affected me (self-centered) or from a concern for another person's relationship with the Lord (God-centered)? Hint: What part of self was threatened or seeking satisfaction?

SELF-SEEKING

Am I more concerned with getting something I have set my sights on or with pleasing God? Does my response stem from not getting the esteem (respect, worth, love) I want, the relationships I want, the security I want, the sex I want, or the future I want?

FRIGHTENED

Is my response birthed from unbelief and distrust (fear) of God, leading me to attempt to meet my own needs, or is it birthed from faith working through love, leading to obedience toward God?

DISHONEST

Dishonesty is rooted in lies. Because we easily believe the lies of the Enemy, we are deceived into believing these desires should be filled by the world and sinful people rather than by our perfect, all-powerful, loving Creator. Am I believing a lie or walking in truth? How am I being deceived?

INCONSIDERATE

Have I considered only myself, or have I really sought to understand the other person and the reason, like me, they tend to act sinfully? Have I considered that they too need God's grace? Have I considered what God might be doing for His kingdom purposes?

The following page will look at how God meets our desires in Himself through faith.

> Delight yourself in the LORD,
> and He will give you the desires of your heart.
> **PSALM 37:4**

Reexamine What Part of Self Was Threatened

SELF-ESTEEM

God has given us a good desire for dignity, worth, and value. However, because of sin we have fallen to a state of depravity. Rather than encouraging self-esteem, we need to be redeemed. Attempts to find worth and value apart from the cross of Jesus Christ are temporary, but God's plan for redeeming people to Himself is eternal. God's love is not conditional. His acceptance is not based on human works and worthiness but on faith in the work of His worthy Son. Our worth comes from God.

PERSONAL RELATIONSHIPS

God created us to live relationally with Him and others. We have a God-given desire to belong. In our fallen state we try to control and define our relationships. By faith we are never alone. God Himself is with us. He adopts us into His family.

MATERIAL SECURITY

When we read Matthew 6:19-34, we realize that God is good, He is in control, and He knows what we need materially. However, He warns us not to lay up treasures on earth because they are easily threatened and do not last. Instead of worrying about those things, we should seek first His eternal kingdom and righteousness. He will provide for us according to His kingdom purposes, in His timing and in His way, as He sees fit.

EMOTIONAL SECURITY

In the perfect garden paradise of Eden before the fall, there was shalom, or peace. We have a God-given desire for peace. Through faith in Jesus Christ, we are given peace with God. We rest behind the mighty fortress of Jesus, where no person or circumstance can rob us of our peace with Him. Even if waves of despair and destruction come crashing in, the Lord is our refuge. We will not be moved, because He cannot be shaken.

SEXUAL RELATIONS/SEXUALITY

We have a God-given desire for pleasure, including sex. God is a God of pleasure, and He gave us senses to enjoy His creation; however, we enjoy it within the boundaries of His instruction. God created sex to be celebrated and enjoyed between a husband and a wife within the covenant of marriage. Outside of that it becomes destructive. There are greater pleasures in God than any mere physical act.

AMBITIONS

Ambitions come from a God-given desire for hope. Apart from the mercy of Christ, we tend to put our hope in things other than God. But God has given us hope: He overcame the world, Satan, sin, and death. We will be raised with Christ and never experience spiritual death again. God demonstrated this miraculous, resurrecting power in Christ on the cross. Our future is secure in Christ, and we can place our hope in Him alone.

REPLANT TRUTH AND RENOUNCE LIES

WEEK 8

You will walk complete phases 3 and 4 in your time together this week (three hours).

REMEMBER: Week 8 has Going Deeper discussion in relation to the week's teaching. The Going Deeper discussion guide can be found on pages 87–88.

REDEMPTIVE VIEWS

The following guides can assist you in replanting life-giving gospel truth in the soil of the participant's heart.

ABUSE AND SUFFERING
ANGER
GUILT AND SHAME
SEX
FEAR
GRIEF AND LOSS

RENOUNCING LIES, VOWS, AND SINFUL PATTERNS

This guide will walk you through a process for renouncing lies, vows, and sinful patterns before seeking to prayerfully uproot them.

PRAYERS OF DELIVERANCE, HEALING, AND BLESSING

This guide deals with the demonic roots of ungodly fruit, including prayer prompts for breaking vows, renouncing lies, and deliverance from sinful patterns.

A Redemptive View of Abuse and Suffering

WASHING WITH THE WORD

After the participant fills out the "Exact nature of my wrongs, faults, and mistakes" section, guide them through the following Scriptures.

1 PETER 2:19-25: This Scripture explains that Jesus was also an abuse victim who suffered righteously and left us an example of how to respond to abuse. Through His wounds we are healed.

PSALM 56:1-11: This Scripture illustrates God's heart for the abused. He has not forgotten them; He has heard their cries.

BIBLICAL TRUTH

Jesus suffered abuse. He was neglected, betrayed, humiliated, stripped naked, beaten, and killed. His experience demonstrates three life-giving truths:

1. Jesus understands. He deeply understands what you have gone through and what you are feeling because He experienced it. He knows your pain.
2. Your abuse does not cause you to sin. Your response comes from the heart. Jesus did not respond to His abuse in sin or vengeance; He "continued entrusting himself to him who judges justly" (1 Pet. 2:23). The more Christ reigns and rules in your heart, the more Christlike your responses will be.
3. God will vindicate you and bring justice. For all those who do not repent, the wrath of God remains on them. And there will be justice.

REDEEMED TRUTH ABOUT ABUSE: Abuse is the misuse of anything. God created all things for His glory, and the misuse of His creation is abuse and ultimately sinful. However, there is a type of abuse that moves beyond what might be considered normative in the Christian life. This abuse is horrifying and horrific, and in keeping with God's heart for the oppressed, the church must be a redemptive instrument in intervening and protecting. We cannot overcome sin independent of God. He has provided the way to overcome sin and its effects through the gospel of Jesus Christ. God does not allow abuse or any other form of suffering in the lives of His children without a redemptive purpose. In Christ, through the Holy Spirit, we can display His supremacy and victory over evil as we rise above sin, shame, and even death.

NEXT: *Use the Renouncing Lies, Vows, and Character Defects guide to renounce any lies, vows, or character defects.*

A Redemptive View of Anger

WASHING WITH THE WORD

After the participant fills out the "Exact nature of my wrongs, faults, and mistakes" section, guide them through the following Scriptures.

ROMANS 12:19-21: We don't have to take revenge (or remain bitter), not because God doesn't care about justice but because He says He will bring perfect justice.

ROMANS 2:1-5: God is righteous in His judgments, and apart from Him we are not. Outside the grace afforded to us through the gospel, we would deserve God's judgment. Many times when we have judged others, we place ourselves under God's judgment, showing that we are guilty of the same sins.

BIBLICAL TRUTH

Jesus got angry. However, His anger was never selfish and always reflected God's heart.

MARK 3:1-6: Jesus was angry in the synagogue because he was grieved at the hardness of men's hearts. His anger was motivated by a love for people and by anger toward sin. Notice that His anger moved Him to act in accordance with God's redemptive purposes.

MARK 11:15-19: Jesus cleared the temple in response to the moneychangers' use of His Father's house for selfish gain. From His love for His Father and zeal for His Father's house, Jesus responded with righteous anger. Notice this was not a reaction to a personal attack but rather a response to an offense against His Father (sin).

God is reconciling the world to Himself through His Son. No sin will go unpunished. Those who have hurt us will either receive the same grace and mercy we have received through the cross or will be judged and spend eternity in torment. Maybe the knowledge of this coming judgment will free you to act as an ambassador of Christ to those who have hurt you.

REDEEMED TRUTH ABOUT ANGER: Anger is an emotional response to a perceived wrong that demands justice. Not all anger is sinful; it can be the appropriate response to injustice. Unrighteous anger is rooted in man's attempts to meet his own idolatrous desires. Righteous anger is aligned with the Holy Spirit and flows from the heart of God in love for that which He cares about, spurring us on to gospel-centered action to eradicate evil and injustice.

NEXT: *Use the Renouncing Lies, Vows, and Character Defects guide to renounce any lies, vows, or character defects.*

A Redemptive View of Sex

WASHING WITH THE WORD

After the participant fills out the "Exact nature of my wrongs, faults, and mistakes" section, guide them through the following Scriptures.

PSALM 51:7; 1 JOHN 3:3: When Christ died on the cross, He not only took our sin but also our shame. In Him we are clean, pure, innocent, and white as snow.

BIBLICAL TRUTH

Sex is a good gift from God, and He created sex to be pleasurable and enjoyable. When you sin sexually, you feel guilt and shame. Because sin taints everything it touches, your mind will begin to attach the feeling of guilt and shame to sex itself, and you may begin to believe sex is dirty or shameful. This is a lie. Only the sin is shameful. No matter how much you have sinned, God can cleanse you of that shame and redeem you to enjoy His gifts.

REDEEMED TRUTH ABOUT SEX: Sex is a beautiful, sacred gift given to us by God. It is to be worshipful but not worshiped. It is to be enjoyed and celebrated within the marriage covenant as a reflection of the gospel and our union with Christ. Any sexual act that occurs outside God's intended design is sexual immorality. Beyond action alone God looks deeper to the desires and motivations of the heart. Only through the gospel will God align our hearts with His purposes for this beautiful, sacred gift.

NEXT: *Use the Renouncing Lies, Vows, and Character Defects guide to renounce any lies, vows, or character defects.*

A Redemptive View of Guilt and Shame

WASHING WITH THE WORD

After the participant fills out the "Exact nature of my wrongs, faults, and mistakes" section, guide them through the following Scriptures.

HEBREWS 4:15-16: This Scripture emphasizes that we have been made clean and holy through Christ. We no longer have to let shame keep us from approaching God.

He knew our dirtiness before we did and still decided to save us. Jesus has willingly taken all the punishment we deserve so that we can approach our Father's throne.

1 JOHN 1:9: This person may have never been loved in their places of greatest shame. You may be the first to hear of the actions they have done or that were done against them. Ask them if there are still details for which they feel shame and invite them to share those details. Use this verse to encourage them that they can be forgiven of their sin and cleansed from the shame of another's sin by bringing it into the light.

BIBLICAL TRUTH

We are guilty when we sin. However, conviction by the Holy Spirit leads to repentance and life, while condemnation leads to hiding and pretending. Because there is no condemnation in Christ, we can approach His throne of grace, knowing He is merciful and forgiving.

Shame has to do with being defiled. This happens when we violate our God-given dignity as image bearers or when we expose our depravity. The good news of the gospel is that when God adopted you into His family and kingdom, He gave you a new name. He gave you dignity in Christ by calling you His daughter or son. The cross of Christ forgives sinners and cleanses victims. We now have an eternal dignity bestowed on us by the King.

REDEEMED TRUTH ABOUT GUILT: Guilt can be both a state and a feeling that occurs when we have violated a law or a moral standard. We can feel guilty and not be guilty (false guilt), or we can be guilty and not feel guilty. False guilt occurs when someone besides God is the lord of our lives and their judgments matter more than His. Not feeling guilt when we are guilty is a sign of a hardened heart. Only the gospel can reconcile a heart of injustice. Life through the Holy Spirit brings conviction when we operate outside God's intended design.

REDEEMED TRUTH ABOUT SHAME: Shame is the intense feeling of being unclean, defiled, and dirty. Closely related to guilt, shame may result from the exposure of a person's own sin and depravity or from sin committed against a person's dignity. Shame is deeply rooted in identity ("I am worthless; I am dirty"). The gospel of Jesus Christ gives us a new identity and a covering for our shame. Even though we may sin or be sinned against, shame no longer rules our lives, because our identity is found in Jesus Christ.

NEXT: *Use the Renouncing Lies, Vows, and Character Defects guide to renounce any lies, vows, or character defects.*

A Redemptive View of Fear

WASHING WITH THE WORD

After the participant fills out the "Exact nature of my wrongs, faults, and mistakes" section, guide them through the following Scriptures.

1 PETER 3:6: The command not to fear does not mean there are not frightful things. God acknowledges the reality of frightening circumstances. However, we can trust that the love of God is more powerful than any danger we face.

PHILIPPIANS 4:4-7: If we believe God will give us everything we need, what do we have to be afraid of?

1 JOHN 4:7-21: The gospel of Jesus Christ removes the curse of sin and the wrath of God and allows us to approach His throne with confidence. Knowing His love for us frees us from self-protection and allows us to sacrificially lay down our lives so that others can know His love. When we walk in fear, we cannot walk in love.

BIBLICAL TRUTH

Our fears are often very revealing. We fear not having the things we lust for or covet. The things we lust for are idols of which we should repent. They may not be bad things in and of themselves, but we should hold them with an open hand, trusting that God will meet our needs according to His kingdom purposes.

Pride is often at the root of our fears. Rather than allowing God to decide what is good for us, we say in our hearts, *This is what is good for me.* When that perceived good thing is threatened, we become fearful.

God is sovereign. God is good. God is love, so His actions always display love. God loves His children. As God's children, we know our Father is mightier than any enemy. All others are small in comparison to Him.

"Fear not" is the most repeated command in the Bible. Not being afraid has little to do with the facts of our circumstances and everything to do with understanding the character of God. Though frightening circumstances are a reality, He is our loving, all-powerful Father who delights in caring for and protecting His children. He supplies all our needs and knows them before we ask. When we find ourselves in fear, we can instead put our thoughts on the faithfulness of God.

REDEEMED TRUTH ABOUT FEAR: Fear is an emotional response to a perceived threat or danger. Spiritually, healthy fear is the fear of the Lord. To fear the Lord is to worship Him alone and is the source of all wisdom and understanding. The absence of the fear of the Lord is the height of foolishness and leads to destruction. Outside the gospel we live our lives from a self-centered fear that seeks to meet our own perceived needs. As the Holy Spirit reveals this foolishness, we come under the compassion and care of our loving Father. He knows best in providing, protecting, and directing our lives according to His plan and purpose for His glory and our good.

NEXT: *Use the Renouncing Lies, Vows, and Character Defects guide to renounce any lies, vows, or character defects.*

A Redemptive View of Grief

WASHING WITH THE WORD

After the participant fills out the "Exact nature of my wrongs, faults, and mistakes" section, guide them through the following Scriptures.

PSALM 10:1; 22:1: If the participant has been repressing anger or frustration, take this time to remind them that they should confess that anger to God. Though resentment against God is a sin, there is a way to confess your feelings of anger and frustration to God in an honest, humble manner. The psalmists were honest with God about feelings of anger, frustration, confusion, and abandonment.

PSALM 34:18-19; MATTHEW 5:4: Use these Scriptures to illustrate that God is always close to us in our suffering. He promises to heal and restore. We must grieve over our loss and allow God to enter and heal our wounds. Encourage the participant to cry out to God.

JOEL 2:25: Read this verse together and talk about the Lord's promise not only to heal but also to restore what has been lost.

BIBLICAL TRUTH

These verses illustrate the hope of the gospel amid our loss. We can confess and cry out to God in our suffering, and He comforts us and promises to restore all that has been lost. There is nothing on earth that we can hold on to eternally, and there is nothing eternal that we can lose in Christ. We are secure in Him. Dealing with loss through sinful ways always brings captivity, but God provides a way of dealing with loss that brings freedom.

REDEEMED TRUTH ABOUT GRIEF: Grief is a natural response to loss and is not sinful. When we grieve, we can do so knowing that we stand in the loving arms of God the Father. Grief in this context is always hopeful because we know that God is making all things new. Grief outside the gospel leaves us to cope through self-generated means and with false hope or no hope at all. Grief can become complicated when we idolize what we lost.

NEXT: *Use the Renouncing Lies, Vows, and Character Defects guide to renounce any lies, vows, or character defects.*

Renouncing Lies, Vows, and Sinful Patterns

It is important to address lies we have agreed with; vows we have made; and sinful patterns of relating to God, ourselves, and others. While we subconsciously believe many lies and flippantly make vows in anger, they hold serious spiritual significance and can tie us to the kingdom of darkness. These lies and vows provide fuel for our lust, pride, and bitterness, as well as a multitude of other sins. The participant's identity as an adopted son or daughter of God is essential to this process and should be your constant message to them. Sin has no power over someone who is in Christ. However, we must renounce ties to the kingdom of darkness, removing any open doors for the Enemy.

SCRIPTURE REVIEW

Lies: Genesis 3:1-5; John 8:31-47
Vows/oaths: Matthew 5:33-37; James 5:12

LIES
I COME OUT OF AGREEMENT WITH ...

Examples:

1. If I had not desired love, then I would not have been abused.

2. I need to look out for myself because no one else is going to.

3. Nobody wants me because I am too messed up. I am unlovable.

TRUTHS
AND I COME INTO AGREEMENT WITH ...

Examples:

1. A wicked human being took advantage of God's child. There is nothing I could have done to prevent that situation. Love is a good gift from God.

2. Only God can protect and defend me. When I try to protect myself, I create a greater mess.

3. The Creator of the universe chose me before the foundation of the earth (see Eph. 1:4). He loves and cherishes me, and His standards matter more than anyone else's.

VOWS/OATHS
I BREAK THE VOW ...

Examples:

1. I will never let anyone get close to me so that I will not get hurt.

2. I will never be put in a shameful situation again.

3. I will not desire anything. I will just be neutral and have no opinions.

I will never _____.

I must always _____.

If I ever _____, then _____.

TRUTHS
AND I COME INTO AGREEMENT WITH ...

Examples:

1. I can trust God to protect me. His love frees me to love others, even if I get hurt.

2. "Those who look to him are radiant, and their faces shall never be ashamed" (Ps. 34:5).

3. "Hope deferred makes the heart sick, but a desire fulfilled is a tree of life" (Prov. 13:12). The Lord gives good gifts, and we can trust Him with our desires. We lack no good thing in Him (see Ps. 34:10).

CHARACTER DEFECTS

As sinners in a fallen world, we are enticed by the Enemy into sinful patterns of relating to God and others (see the list of spiritual defects in appendix E). Independent of God we seek to cope, and this self-effort leads to greater chaos. Freedom is found in the kingdom of God through His Son. We must renounce our former ways and submit all areas of our lives to His kingdom purposes, under the reign and rule of our great King, Jesus.

Prayers of Deliverance, Healing, and Blessing

This is a time to come before the Lord; lay our lives at His feet; and ask Him to bring freedom, healing, and blessing. We must start by offering our lives completely to Him, asking Him to make us useful to Him, according to His will and His kingdom purposes. We renounce lies; break vows; and pray that He will deliver us from sinful patterns of relating to Him, ourselves, the creation, and one another in the name of Christ and by His authority. This time of prayer should be devoted to mental, emotional, spiritual, relational, and physical healing.

The participant should share what God revealed through the assessments about significant patterns of sinful behavior, thoughts, and attitudes. They should identify generational patterns of sin and specific areas in which they desire deliverance from bondage and healing from past wounds.

As Jesus' model prayer teaches us (see Matt. 6:9-13), we must first pray for God's name to be lifted up, for His kingdom to come, and for His will to be done. Accordingly, we must lay down our name, our kingdom, and our will to His.

PRAYER PROMPTS

PRAYER TO COME UNDER HIS AUTHORITY

Heavenly Father, I have now seen how I have lived by the ways of the world and have lived for my kingdom, my name, and my will. I now renounce those ways and offer myself completely to You to be utilized for Your kingdom plan and purposes.

PRAYER FOR PROVISION, PROTECTION, AND DIRECTION

Heavenly Father, give us this day what we need to accomplish Your kingdom purposes. Protect us from any interference by the Enemy and his servants, works, and effects during our time of prayer. You are greater than he who is in the world.

PRAYER TO RENOUNCE SPECIFIC LIES
(TO BE PRAYED OVER EACH LIE)

Loving Father, please forgive me for believing the lie that _____.
I renounce that lie and come into agreement with the truth that _____.

PRAYER TO BREAK VOWS (TO BE PRAYED OVER EACH VOW)

Loving Father, in my distress I have vowed to/to never _____. In doing so, I have alienated myself from You and sought to keep myself from harm. I have placed myself under the Devil's authority and have given him a foothold in my life. I now break that vow by Christ's authority and come to You as my protector. I trust that You will give me grace to overcome all the Enemy's influence.

PRAYER FOR DELIVERANCE

- The participant should understand the prayer and pray in agreement as he or she is prayed over.
- This time of prayer is to engage in spiritual battle at the level of personal entanglement and not beyond that.

Heavenly Father, for Your namesake and according to Your love and mercy, we ask that You will deliver _____ from any demonic influence that is tempting him/her to _____ so that he/she may freely serve You and Your kingdom. He/she has agreed with Your adversary and now renounces his ways. Spirit of _____, we command you by the authority of the Holy Spirit to release _____ at once. We command you to go directly without incident to the feet of Jesus, where He will deal with you according to His eternal purposes. We command you never to return to _____ or to any of his/her family, friends, or loved ones. In the name of Jesus, we bind you and all spirits that may be assigned with you, and we command you to go. Lord God, we ask You to fill the places previously occupied by the Enemy with the Holy Spirit and bless _____ in the name of Jesus Christ.

ELEMENTS OF THIS PRAYER

- Acknowledge by what power and authority we approach the throne of God.
- Request deliverance from a specific stronghold.
- Come with the purposes of using freedom to be utilized for God's kingdom.
- Command the spirit to release the individual by the authority of Christ and the power of the Holy Spirit.
- Instruct the spirit to go to Jesus without incident.
- Bind all those assigned with this spirit together and command them to go and never return to the individual or his/her family, friends, or loved ones.
- Pray for the Holy Spirit to fill this person.
- Pray for blessing.

Truly, I say to you, whoever says to this mountain, "Be taken up and thrown into the sea," and does not doubt in his heart, but believes that what he says will come to pass, it will be done for him. Therefore I tell you, whatever you ask in prayer, believe that you have received it, and it will be yours.

MARK 11:23-24

Which one of you, if his son asks him for bread, will give him a stone? Or if he asks for a fish, will give him a serpent? If you then, who are evil, know how to give good gifts to your children, how much more will your Father who is in heaven give good things to those who ask him!

MATTHEW 7:9-11

Behold, I have given you authority to tread on serpents and scorpions, and over all the power of the enemy, and nothing shall hurt you.

LUKE 10:19

GETTING TO THE ROOTS: OFFERING AND ASKING

▌ COMPLETE PHASES 3 & 4 (SEE PAGES 71–86).

▌ PRAY, LOVE, ASK, & LISTEN

Ask whether the mentee has questions about the homework since the previous meeting.

Ask what the mentee learned about God and himself or herself this week.

Discuss the Going Deeper questions, taking notes as needed (this is a time to listen).

1. Internal ruling desires lead to fights and quarrels. What desires tend to rule your heart and spark anger?
2. What do you turn to instead of God to fulfill your desires?
3. How do you attempt to satisfy your desire for peace?
4. Where do you typically look for hope?
5. Where do you find value, worth, and significance?
6. We all have an innate desire to belong to something bigger than ourselves. Historically, what lengths have you gone to in order to belong? Today what do you have in common with those who are closest to you?
7. To what lengths have you gone to meet your material needs? Have you ever sinned to meet those needs?
8. When we withhold an area of our lives from Christ and His lordship (authority), to whom do we give authority by default?
9. What character defects do you need to surrender to Jesus, trusting Him to provide the grace you need?
10. Are there areas of your life in which you still feel enslaved?
11. Are there physical, emotional, spiritual, or relational wounds that you desire Jesus to heal?
12. What gospel truths and gospel pursuits affected you most this week?

Review the redeemed truth for steps 6 and 7 (see appendix A).

▌ SPEAK, LEAD, REMIND, & PRAY

NOTES

ENCOURAGE TO FAITHFUL ACTION

Behold, a lawyer stood up to put him to the test, saying, "Teacher, what shall I do to inherit eternal life?" He said to him, "What is written in the Law? How do you read it?" And he answered, "You shall love the Lord your God with all your heart and with all your soul and with all your strength and with all your mind, and your neighbor as yourself."

LUKE 10:25-27

WEEKS 9–12

There is no template or to-do list that will lead to fullness of life other than obedience to the incarnate Word of God, as directed by the Holy Spirit, rooted in love for the person and work of Jesus Christ. Scripture tells us:

In Christ Jesus neither circumcision nor uncircumcision counts for anything, but only faith working through love.

GALATIANS 5:6

For each person, faith must express itself in action done from a regenerate heart of love for Jesus. These are not works to become righteous but rather are expressions of the new heart and righteousness given to us in Christ.

LOVING GOD (VERTICAL)

- Meeting with God through the spiritual disciplines so that we can know Him and the power of His resurrection
- Expressions of gratitude—enjoying His gifts, joining His ministry, and serving in His church
- Stoking the flames of gospel-centered worship—expressions of the heart, both individually and corporately
- Obedience to His statutes—learning, doing, and sharing with others
- Continued mortification of sin

LOVING OTHERS AND SELF (HORIZONTAL)

- Making disciples for Christ
- Reflecting the heart of God and the mind of Christ
- Gospel-centered service
- Gospel-empowered ministry and mission
- Gospel-centered community
- Seeking reconciliation for sins committed
- Taking care of your body, the temple of God
- Asking your Father in heaven for what you need

You and the participant should agree on a plan of action for seeking reconciliation and amends. This includes making a list of people whom participants owe amends or forgiveness. Some other ideas for pursuing joy in Christ include key Scriptures to combat lies, unbelief, and fears; an ongoing study and meditation plan; instruction in prayer and the pursuit of biblical community; and helping participants consider, plan, and ask the Lord how He can utilize them in making disciples.

Seeking Reconciliation and Amends

The work of amends displays God as a just God who cares about His children and is intent on bringing justice to the oppressed. We arrive at this justice through the reconciliation of our hearts to His through the gospel of grace, which cures what the law cannot. The gospel alone transforms the heart of injustice.

TRADITIONAL STEP 8: We made a list of all persons we had harmed and became willing to make amends to them all.

TRADITIONAL STEP 9: We made direct amends to such people whenever possible, except when to do so would injure them or others.

The light of Christ shines into our hearts. It exposes darkness while providing the hope of restoration through the reconciling work of Jesus Christ. He Himself demonstrates the power and possibility of overcoming sin, suffering, and death. For those of us who are forgiven by God and are now living as His ambassadors, this process allows us to bring light and hope to a dark world. We are to use all of our energy and resources to glorify His name. Confessing our wrongs with a sincere desire to make things right is an opportunity to testify to the character of God as both just and merciful. Restitution is often a forgotten component of repentance; however, a repentant heart, in response to God's grace, is willing to forsake any worldly costs because of the promise of Christ for all eternity.

WILLINGNESS VERSUS WISDOM

With respect to making amends, step 8 speaks to willingness, and step 9 speaks to wisdom. We must be willing to make amends but use wisdom in making them. For example, it might not be wise to make direct amends in dangerous situations. It might not be wise to look up every person you have ever had a sexual experience with and invite them to coffee. It might not be wise to meet with a married person of the opposite sex without his or her spouse. You should use wisdom and sensitivity in the words you choose and consider your audience in acknowledging your wrongs. It might not be wise to confess sinful thoughts or attitudes to someone who is unaware that you thought of them that way. It might not be wise to force an amends before a person is willing to receive it. Remember, the Holy Spirit leads. He will impress on you whom to approach, direct you when to approach, and may even bring some unexpected opportunities to make peace.

The exception—"except when to do so would injure them or others"—is often used as a cover-up for unwillingness. For example, we should not use this exception as an excuse not to confess adultery, claiming it would hurt the other person too much. Confession allows true healing to occur rather than covering up the sin that disrupts fellowship. As long as secrets remain, we cannot have true fellowship. If we do not confess adultery, a marriage is based on deceit. In confessing situations that include sexual sin, consider sparing the other person specific details that may make healing unnecessarily difficult.

A TEMPLATE FOR MAKING AMENDS

Peacemaker Ministries suggests the seven A's of confession, which we adapted for *Steps:*
1. Address those affected.
2. Avoid excusing your wrongs or being overly dramatic in an attempt to evoke pity.
3. Admit specific attitudes and actions.
4. Acknowledge the hurt and express regret for harm caused.
5. Accept the consequences and be willing to make restitution.
6. Accompany confession with altered attitudes and actions.
7. Ask for forgiveness.[1]

Often we already know what we need to do to make things right. If we owe someone money, we may be prepared to pay them with interest. Sometimes we are not in a position to make full restitution at that point, but we can give something and make arrangements for future payments.

For those of us who have misused religion, the Bible, or God to justify a sinful attitude or behavior, it is wise to acknowledge ways we have been wrong.

EXAMPLE: "I am grateful that God has granted me this opportunity to speak with you today. The gospel of Jesus Christ has had a profound effect on my life. He has both provided me hope and exposed the depths of my sin. In light of His work in my life, I deeply regret how my sinful attitudes and actions have affected you. I am here to ask for your forgiveness. [Explain how you wronged this person.] I regret the harm I have caused you. I know I cannot heal the wounds I have caused, but I serve a God who can. Will you forgive me? What can I do to make this situation right?"

CAUTION

We can go only as far as God allows us. If making a situation right is contrary to the will of God in your life, you may not sin against Him to make amends to someone.

REDEEMED TRUTH FROM STEPS 8 & 9: Relationships break down because of sin. If there were no sin in the world, relationships would work harmoniously, evidenced by love and unity. Division among God's people provides opportunities to identify sin and purify the body. The gospel of Jesus Christ brings about justice in a way that the law cannot by inwardly reconciling the very heart of injustice to God. As those forgiven by God, we can humbly approach those affected by our sin and make amends. This change of heart brings glory to God by demonstrating the power of the gospel and reflecting His heart in bringing justice through His reconciled people.

TYPES OF RECONCILIATION

RELATIONAL: In rebellion against God's created order, we have lived for ourselves and have used people for our selfish desires. Now that we are reconciled to God, we desire to make amends for harm done through our selfish ambitions.

LEGAL: At times our self-seeking behavior has led us not only to rebel against God but also to break laws intended to uphold and safeguard society. Setting things right may mean making amends and possibly restitution for harm done.

PROFESSIONAL: We may not have been faithful to the responsibilities entrusted to us professionally.

FINANCIAL: Monetary compensation may be required to make things right.

RELIGIOUS/SPIRITUAL: We may need to confess and ask for forgiveness for misleading someone spiritually.

LIVING: A person may not be willing to hear from us, in which case we must demonstrate the transformative effects of the gospel in our lives by living faithfully and responsibly.

1. Adapted from "Seven A's of Confession," *Peacemaker Ministries* [online], 22 September 2014 [cited 5 October 2015]. Available from the Internet: *http://peacemaker.net/project/seven-as-of-confession/*.

FAITHFUL ACTION

PEACEMAKING, PART I: RECONCILING AND AMENDING

■ **BEGIN PHASE 5 (SEE PAGE 87–90).**

■ **PRAY, LOVE, ASK, & LISTEN**

Ask whether the mentee has questions about the homework since the previous meeting.
Ask what the mentee learned about God and himself or herself this week.
Discuss the Going Deeper questions, taking notes as needed (this is a time to listen).

1. How does fear prevent you from loving others as Christ does? Give specific examples from your life (confronting difficult situations, willingness to share your faith, etc.).
2. Have you ever used your knowledge and intellect as a source of pride to beat people down rather than build them up? Give examples.
3. Describe times when your idolatry has distorted your judgment in acting according to God's will.
4. In Matthew 5:23-24 the Lord taught the importance of being reconciled prior to bringing our gifts before the altar. Describe situations in which you offended someone with whom you need to be reconciled.
5. Are there people or institutions to whom you are unwilling to confess and make restitution? Be specific.

Review the redeemed truth for steps 8 and 9 (see appendix A).

■ **SPEAK, LEAD, REMIND, & PRAY**

NOTES

PEACEMAKING, PART 2: CONFRONTING AND FORGIVING

■ **COMPLETE PHASE 5 (SEE PAGE 87–90).**

■ **PRAY, LOVE, ASK, & LISTEN**

Ask whether the mentee has questions about the homework since the previous meeting.
Ask what the mentee learned about God and himself or herself this week.
Discuss the Going Deeper questions, taking notes as needed (this is a time to listen).

1. As people repent and confess sin to us, we need to be ready to offer forgiveness. Our forgiveness is evidence that Christ's forgiveness has transformed our hearts and that we want them to be reconciled to God. Prayerfully consider and list the names of people whom you might have difficulty forgiving.
2. Are there brothers or sisters in Christ who may have sinned against you and continue to walk in significant unrepentant sin? Prayerfully consider how God is calling you to forgive these people for the sin they committed against you.
3. Now that bitterness, fear, and shame no longer rule you, are there people outside the body of Christ who may have hurt you and need to be offered peace with God through the blood of Christ?
4. Where are you stuck? Discuss with your group any situations in which you are unwilling to make amends, forgive, confront, or share the gospel. Why?
5. Discuss any fears you have in making amends, forgiving, confronting someone's sin, or sharing the hope of the gospel. Why are you afraid?
6. Are there any relationships you believe are beyond repair?
7. Spend time in prayer as a group, specifically for those situations.
8. Discuss any other questions or issues you are facing.

Review the redeemed truth for steps 8 and 9 (see appendix A).

■ **SPEAK, LEAD, REMIND, & PRAY**

NOTES

PERSEVERING AND PURSUING

■ PRAY, LOVE, ASK, & LISTEN

Ask whether the mentee has questions about the homework since the previous meeting.

Ask what the mentee learned about God and himself or herself this week.

Discuss the Going Deeper questions, taking notes as needed (this is a time to listen).

1. What sin or weight do you need to lay aside in order to run the race well?
2. What trials are you facing in your life? In what ways are you tempted to preempt God's purposes of sanctification while under trial?
3. How do you know when you are walking by the Spirit? How does this walk express itself in your life with the people and circumstances you encounter (family, coworkers, children, prayer life, etc.)?
4. What would obedience to Christ look like in your life?
5. When you are thirsting in the wilderness, where do you turn for satisfaction? What does this response reveal about your heart?
6. On what do you tend to obsess, fantasize, meditate, or dwell? Be specific. What is the result (fear, anxiety, depression, worship, praise, joy, etc.)?
7. What stirs your affection for Christ?
8. Being undisciplined leads to laziness or apathy. How disciplined are you in engaging spiritual disciplines daily? If you are undisciplined, why?
9. What does a disciplined life look like specifically for you?
10. What are your goals and motivations for living a disciplined life?
11. Are there things you need to say no to in order to love the Lord and in turn love your spouse, family, friends, neighbors, and coworkers?

Review the redeemed truth for steps 10 and 11 (see appendix A).

■ SPEAK, LEAD, REMIND, & PRAY

■ AFTER-CARE & NEXT STEPS

Work with your mentee's leader to develop an after-care plan and to identify next steps.

NOTES

WEEK 12

THE JOY OF MAKING MUCH OF HIS NAME

■ PRAY, LOVE, ASK, & LISTEN

Ask whether the mentee has questions about the homework since the previous meeting.

Ask what the mentee learned about God and himself or herself this week.

Discuss the Going Deeper questions, taking notes as needed (this is a time to listen).

1. How has God blessed you so that you can be a blessing to others?
2. How has God gifted you with spiritual gifts from the Holy Spirit? How will you use those gifts to serve and build up the body of Christ? Be specific.
3. How will you use your testimony of God's grace to guide others toward Christ?
4. Where has God placed you to serve? How do you think others would describe your heart for service?
5. God has called us to make disciples. How will you apply what you have learned through this discipleship process to make disciples for Christ?
6. Acts 17 shows us, through Paul's missionary experiences, that God places us at the exact time and place where He wants to use us. How are you living missionally within your community?
7. How will you continue to practice all you have learned through the *Steps* process? Who will keep you accountable?
8. With what attitude will you engage or reengage with the world around you? Is there any obstacle or excuse that would keep you from doing so?
9. The Book of Joshua recounts the Lord's powerful deliverance of the promised land to the Israelites. As they stepped out in faith, He held back the raging waters of the Jordan River so that they could cross to safety. The Israelites picked up stones from the riverbed to remind them of the Lord's faithfulness. As you have stepped out in faith, in what ways has God demonstrated His faithfulness during this particular season of your life?

Review the redeemed truth for step 12 (see appendix A).

■ SPEAK, LEAD, REMIND, & PRAY

■ AFTER-CARE & NEXT STEPS

Work with your mentee's leader to develop an after-care plan and to identify next steps.

NOTES

REDEEMING THE 12 STEPS THROUGH THE GOSPEL

Step 1: We admitted we were powerless over our addictions and compulsive behaviors—that our lives had become unmanageable.

Redeemed truth from step 1: Man, in relationship to his Creator, has fallen from a place of dignity, humility, and dependence to a state of depravity, pride, and rebellion. This has led to unfathomable suffering. Any attempts on our own to redeem ourselves are futile, only increasing the problem of independence and self-sufficiency. Any perceived success leads only to empty vanity. Apart from Christ, we are powerless to overcome sin, and our attempts to control it only increase our chaos.

Step 2: We came to believe that a power greater than ourselves could restore us to sanity.

Redeemed truth from step 2: God lovingly intervened into our chaos and provided a remedy for the insanity of sin and the way back into fellowship with Him. We believe that by grace through faith in Jesus Christ, we can be redeemed.

Step 3: We made a decision to turn our will and our lives over to the care of God, as you understand Him.

Redeemed truth from step 3: Through the Holy Spirit's illumination of our desperate and helpless condition before God and from the hope that comes through the gospel of Jesus Christ, we step out in faith and repent as an act of worship and obedience, surrendering our will and entrusting our lives to Christ's care and control. We are reborn spiritually and rescued from the domain of darkness and brought into the kingdom of light, where we now live as a part of Christ's ever-advancing kingdom.

Step 4: We made a searching and fearless moral assessment of ourselves.

Redeemed truth from step 4: .As children of God armed with the Holy Spirit and standing firm in the gospel, we engage in the spiritual battle over the reign and rule of our hearts. God set us apart for holiness, and we look to put to death the areas of our lives that keep us from reflecting Jesus Christ to a dark and dying world. We first examine the fruit in our lives (or moral symptoms). As we move through the assessment process, we will uncover the roots of any ungodly fruit (pride and idolatry) that drive our ungodly thoughts, actions, and emotions

Step 5: We admitted before God, ourselves, and another human being the exact nature of our wrongs.

Redeemed truth from step 5: Under the covering of God's grace, we step out in faith, leaving behind our old, self-protective ways of covering sin and hiding from God. We prayerfully come into the light, confessing our sins before God and to one another so that we may be healed.

Step 6: We are entirely ready to have God remove all these defects of character.

Step 7: We humbly asked Him to remove our shortcomings.

Redeemed truth from steps 6 & 7: In attempting to live independent of God, we have developed dysfunctional (sinful) patterns of coping. After careful examination we have begun to see the demonic roots of our slavery to these sinful patterns. We desire freedom. We renounce our former ways; offer ourselves to God; and, under the waterfall of His grace, ask Him to deliver and heal us by the authority of Christ and the power of the Holy Spirit. We also pray for blessing and the empowerment of the Holy Spirit to live life according to His kingdom purposes.

Step 8: We made a list of all persons we had harmed and became willing to make amends to them all.

Step 9: We made direct amends to such people whenever possible, except when to do so would injure them or others.

Redeemed truth from steps 8 & 9: Relationships break down because of sin. If there were no sin in the world, relationships would work harmoniously, evidenced by love and unity. Division among God's people provides opportunities to identify sin and purify the body. The gospel of Jesus Christ brings about justice in a way that the law cannot by inwardly reconciling the very heart of injustice to God. As those forgiven by God, we can humbly approach those affected by our sin and make amends. This change of heart brings glory to God by demonstrating the power of the gospel and reflecting His heart in bringing justice through His reconciled people.

Additional redeemed truth from steps 8 & 9: As ambassadors of Christ, we are to be instruments of grace as we confront those who sin against us. We hand our offenses over to God and extend eager forgiveness to those who ask for it. And in this way, fellowship with God and among His people is preserved.

Step 10: We continued to take personal inventory and, when we were wrong, promptly admitted it.

Step 11: We sought through prayer and meditation to improve our conscious contact with God, praying only for the knowledge of His will and the power to carry that out.

Redeemed truth from steps 10 & 11: We continue in the fear of the Lord, putting to death those things that rob our affections for Christ while persevering in our loving and joyful obedience to Him. We return to the Lord quickly with an attitude of repentance, when out of step with the Spirit, as we're trained in godliness and grow spiritually. Since He is our ultimate treasure, we seek to know Him and fill ourselves with those things that stir our affections for Him. We practice spiritual disciplines so that our hearts, so prone to wander, might stay in rhythm with His.

Step 12: Having had a spiritual experience as the result of these steps, we try to carry this message to others and to practice these principles in all our affairs.

Redeemed truth from step 12: Before the foundations of the earth, God chose us, the church, to live as messengers of reconciliation to a lost and dying world, bearing witness to His wisdom and power through the gospel of Jesus Christ. It is our joy-filled worship to make much of His name, empowered by the Holy Spirit in bringing a comprehensive gospel demonstrated by our deeds and proclaimed by our words, with the goal of making disciples for Jesus Christ. In this same way, we incarnate Christ, being His hands and feet on the earth.

APPENDIX B

THE CHARACTER OF GOD

ATTRIBUTE	DESCRIPTION	KEY SCRIPTURES
God is just.	God is right to punish sin.	
God is worthy.	Only God deserves all glory.	
God is generous.	God gives what is best.	
God is Provider.	God meets the needs of His children.	
God is merciful.	God does not give His children the punishment they deserve.	
God is loving.	God does what is best.	
Got is attentive.	God hears and responds to the prayers of His children.	
God is Deliverer.	God rescues His children.	
God is compassionate.	God sees, cares, and acts when His children are in need.	

APPENDIX C

THE IDENTITY OF A BELIEVER IN UNION WITH JESUS CHRIST

IDENTITY IN CHRIST

Matthew 5:13	I am the salt of the earth.
Matthew 5:14	I am the light of the world.
John 1:12	I am a child of God.
John 15	I am part of the true vine, a branch of Christ's life.
John 15:15	I am a friend of God.
John 15:16	I am chosen and appointed to bear fruit.
Romans 6:5	I am resurrected to new life.
Romans 6:18	I am a slave to righteousness.
Romans 6:22	I am enslaved to God.
Romans 8:14	I am a son of God.
Romans 8:17	I am a joint heir with Christ, sharing his inheritance.
1 Corinthians 6:19	I am the dwelling place of God.
1 Corinthians 6:19	I am united to the Lord.
1 Corinthians 12:27	I am a member of Christ's body.
1 Corinthians 15:10	I am what I am, by God's grace.

2 Corinthians 5:17	I am a new creation.
2 Corinthians 5:18-19	I am reconciled to God.
Galatians 3:29	I am the seed of Abraham.
Galatians 4:6-7	I am an heir of God since I am a son of God.
Ephesians 1:1	I am a saint.
Ephesians 1:3	I am blessed with every spiritual blessing.
Ephesians 2:10	I am God's workmanship, made to do good works.
Ephesians 2:11	I am a fellow citizen of God's family.
Ephesians 4:1	I am a prisoner of Christ.
Ephesians 4:24	I am righteous and holy.
Philippians 3:20	I am a citizen of heaven.
Colossians 3:3	I am hidden with Christ in God.
Colossians 3:4	I am an expression of the life of Christ.
Colossians 3:12	I am chosen of God, holy and dearly loved.
1 Thessalonians 5:5	I am a child of light and not darkness.
Titus 3:7	I am an heir to eternal life.
Hebrews 3:1	I am a holy partaker of a heavenly calling.
1 Peter 2:5	I am a living stone in God's spiritual house.
1 Peter 2:9	I am a member of a chosen race, a holy nation.
1 Peter 2:9-10	I am a priest.
1 Peter 2:11	I am an alien and a stranger to the world.
1 Peter 5:8	I am an enemy of the Devil.
2 Peter 1:3	I am participating in the divine nature.
1 John 5:18	I am born of God, and the Devil cannot touch me.

IDENTITY APART FROM CHRIST

Genesis 6:5	I am wicked and evil.
Isaiah 59:2	I am separated from God.
Isaiah 64:6	I am filthy and stained.
John 8:34	I am a slave to sin.
Romans 1:18	I am under the wrath of God.
Romans 3:10	I am not good.
Romans 3:23	I am falling short of the glory of God.
Romans 5:26	I am guilty and condemned.
2 Corinthians 4:4	I am blind to the truth.
2 Corinthians 11:3	I am deceived.
Ephesians 2:1	I am dead in my sins.
Ephesians 2:2	I am in bondage to Satan.
Ephesians 4:18	I am hard-hearted.
James 2:10	I am a lawbreaker.
James 4:4	I am an enemy of God.

GOD'S PROMISES TO A BELIEVER

Matthew 6:25-30	God will provide for your needs.
Matthew 11:28-30	Rest in Christ.
Matthew 21:22	Ask in His name, and you will receive.
Matthew 24:9-14	Persecution is coming.
Matthew 26:29	He is waiting to eat with you.
Matthew 28:20	He is with us always, to the end of age.
Mark 16:16	Whoever believes and is baptized will be saved.
Luke 12:27-34	He knows what you need; seek His kingdom, and what you need will be provided.
John 14:1-4	Jesus is preparing a place for you.
John 14:13-14	Ask in Jesus' name, and He will do it so that the Father can be glorified in the Son.
John 14:27	He gives us His peace.
John 15:7-8	If you remain in Him, ask whatever you want.
John 15:5	If you remain in Christ, you will produce fruit.
John 16:13-15	The Holy Spirit will guide you into all truth.
John 16:23-24	Ask the Father in Jesus' name, and it will be given so that your joy may be full.
Acts 1:8	You will receive power when the Holy Spirit comes.
Acts 1:38-39	The promise is for you, the believer.
Romans 6:14	Sin will not rule over you.
Romans 8:27	The Holy Spirit intercedes for the saints according to the will of God.
Romans 8:34	Jesus is at the right hand of the Father interceding for you.
Romans 8:39	Nothing will have the power to separate you from the love of God in Jesus Christ.
1 Corinthians 1:8	He will strengthen you till the end.
1 Corinthians 2:13	The Holy Spirit will teach you.
1 Corinthians 2:16	You have been given the mind of Christ.
1 Corinthians 10:13	God will not allow you to be tempted beyond what you are able, and He will provide a way out.
1 Corinthians 15:52-57	You will be raised into an incorruptible immortal body at the resurrection of the dead.
2 Corinthians 3:18	You are being transformed into the image of Christ.
Philippians 1:6	He who started a good work in you will complete it.
Philippians 3:21-22	He will transform the body of our humble condition into the likeness of His glorious body.
Philippians 4:7	The peace of God will guard your heart and mind in Jesus Christ.

1 Thessalonians 5:24	He who calls you is faithful, who will also do it.
2 Thessalonians 3:3	The lord is faithful and will strengthen and guard you from the Evil One.
Titus 3: 6-7	He has abundantly poured out His Spirit on us through Jesus, and we are heirs to the hope of eternal life.
Hebrews 7:25	He is able to save all who come to Him, and He always intercedes for them.
Hebrews 8:8-12	God will never again remember your sins.
Hebrews 10:16-17	In the new covenant God will never again remember your sins or your lawless acts.
Hebrews 13:5	God will never leave or forsake you.
1 Peter 1:3-5	Inheritance is imperishable, undefiled, uncorrupted, unfading, kept in heaven for you.
1 Peter 2:10	You are now a part of God's people.
Revelation 21:1-7	God will dwell with us and wipe away every tear, and death will no longer exist.

APPENDIX E

DEFINITIONS OF CHARACTER DEFECTS

Abuse: To treat wrongly or harmfully

Addiction: The condition of being habitually or compulsively occupied with or involved in something

Adultery: Voluntary sexual intercourse between a married person and a partner other than the lawful spouse

Anger: A strong feeling of displeasure or hostility

Anxiety: A state of apprehension, uncertainty, and fear resulting from the anticipation of a realistic or fantasized threatening event or situation, often impairing physical and psychological functioning

Bitterness: Unresolved anger and ill will

Bigotry: Hatred of people who are different from me in a clearly definable way, such as race, gender, or political affiliation

Busyness/overscheduling: Planning too many activities in my life so that I do not have time to think about my life

Condemnation: Strong displeasure or judgment

Coveting: Having a desire for another's possessions, power, wealth, or relationships

Critical: Judging, blaming, or finding fault with someone or something

Death/suicide: Enticement to take one's own life or fanaticizing about death

Defeated: Believing there is no hope of victory

Defensive/self-justification: Giving a good reason for my actions; showing my behavior to be just or right; clearing myself from blame for my actions or attitudes

Denial: A false systems of beliefs that are not based on reality; self-protecting behavior that keeps me from honestly facing the truth

Deceitful: Lying, cheating, or stealing; not upright in my dealings with people

Depression: The condition of being lowered in spirit; dejected

Detachment: To remove from association (from self or others); dissociation

Doubt: To be undecided or skeptical

Entitlement: Deserving of rights or benefits

Envy: Wishing to have something someone else has; disliking someone who has more than I do

Fear: A feeling that makes you turn away or run from something

Gluttony: Excess in any area, particularly in eating or drinking; greedy

Gossiping: Idle talk, not always true, about other people and their lives

Grandiosity: Having or showing too great an opinion of my importance

Greed: Wanting more than my fair share

Guilt: Remorseful awareness of having done something wrong

Hate: A feeling of intense anger or bitterness; extreme dislike toward someone; a feeling of intense ill will toward another person

Hoarding: Saving money of things in excess; storing up more than could reasonably be used

Impatience: Annoyance because of delay or opposition

Intolerance: Unwillingness to allow others to have opinions or beliefs that are different from mine

Jealousy: Dislike or fear of rivals; envy; anxious or suspicious watchfulness

Lack of trust: Not being able to trust; not being able to depend on someone or something; doubt; lack in belief in God's goodness

Laziness: Dislike of work; unwillingness to work or be active

Legalism: Strict adherence to rules of conduct without regard to the principles behind them; dependence on my behavior for my sense of self-worth

Licentiousness: Lacking moral discipline or ignoring legal restraint

Lust: Strong desire; unhealthy appetite of desire, especially in the area of sexual indulgences

Lying: Not telling the truth; exaggerating; boasting

Mania: An excessively elevated sense of enthusiasm, interest, or desire; a craze

Minimizing: Making excuses for or making less of my behavior to make myself and others think I am not "that bad"

Negative thinking: Always thinking on the bad side of a situation; refusing to see good in anything that happens; not looking at things from God's point of view

Obsession: Overwhelming attention to a particular thought, action, or person that you cannot escape

Oppression: The act of subjugating by cruelty or force or the state of being subjugated this way

Passivity: Accepting ideas without giving them any thought; failing to act when action is needed

People pleasing: Doing activities based on the positive reactions of people around me; making myself feel better by getting the approval of someone else

Perfectionism: Working to arrange my life so that everything and everyone in it is faultless, according to my standards

Pettiness: Focusing on the small, meaningless things in my life; giving those things more importance than they deserve

Phoniness: Deceiving; being insincere; not being genuine; also includes emotional phoniness

Pride: Too high opinion of myself; high opinion of my worth or possessions

Procrastination: Putting off to a future date something I feel I should have done sooner to avoid unpleasant or undesirable consequences

Quarrelsome: Too quick to find fault; fond of fighting and disputing

Resentment: Sulking; vindictiveness (getting even); reliving emotional hurts and pain

Sarcasm: A sneering or cutting remark; the act of making fun of someone to hurt their feelings; harsh or bitter irony

Self-pity: To feel sorry for myself, to live in regret of my past actions; continually reviewing my miseries, often blaming others for my troubles

Self-centeredness: Being overly concerned with my welfare or interests; having little or no concern for others; thinking what I want is the most important thing

Selfishness: Caring too much for myself and too little for those around me

Shame: A painful emotion caused by a strong sense of guilt, embarrassment, unworthiness, or disgrace

Undisciplined: Untrained; lack of order; lack of self control; disobedient; impulsive

Vulgar thinking: Immoral thinking about things that are unhealthy or immoral; making a practice of dwelling on these thoughts for pleasure or comfort

APPENDIX F

THE INSANITY CYCLE OF SIN

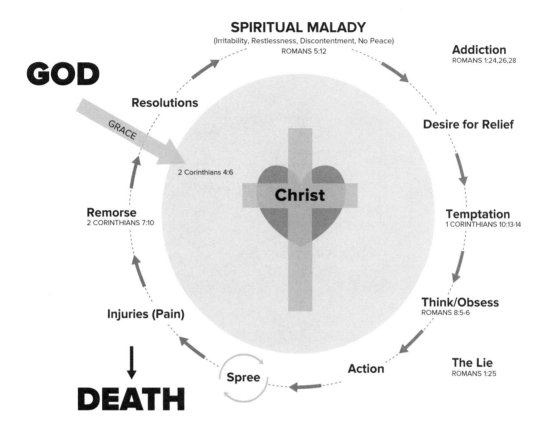

THE THREE CIRCLES: A GOD-CENTERED LIFE

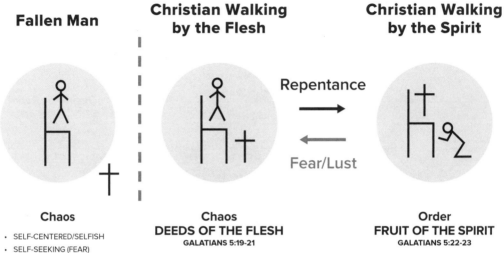

Fallen Man

Christian Walking by the Flesh

Christian Walking by the Spirit

Repentance

Fear/Lust

Chaos

- SELF-CENTERED/SELFISH
- SELF-SEEKING (FEAR)
- SELF-RELIANT (POWER)
- OBSESSED WITH CONTROL, OTHERS, CIRCUMSTANCES
- SPIRITUAL—ALIVE TO SIN, DEAD TO GOD

Chaos
DEEDS OF THE FLESH
GALATIANS 5:19-21

Order
FRUIT OF THE SPIRIT
GALATIANS 5:22-23

- GOD-CENTERED SERVANT
- GOD-PLEASING (FAITH)
- DEPENDENT ON MY CREATOR
- SURRENDERED TO GOD'S SOVEREIGNTY

Adapted from Campus Crusade for Christ.